Photography by Ray Main

vinny lee

101 IDEAS

colour

quadrille

Editorial Director Jane O'Shea
Art Director Helen Lewis
Designer Paul Welti
Project Editor Hilary Mandleberg
Production Rebecca Short

Photography Ray Main

First published in 2005 by
Quadrille Publishing Limited
Alhambra House
27–31 Charing Cross Road
London WC2H 0LS

British Library Cataloguing-in-Publication
Data. A catalogue record for this book is
available from the British Library.

ISBN 1-84400-131-8

Every effort has been made to ensure the
accuracy of the information in this book. In no
circumstances can the publisher or the author
accept any liability for any loss, injury or
damage of any kind resulting from any error
in or omission from the information contained
in this book.

Printed in China

contents

part one
the big picture

part one

the big picture

1 what is colour?

Colours in the visible spectrum are dependent on light. Go back to your schooldays and think of a prism or a rainbow and you'll remember that each colour has a different wavelength – red has the longest and violet the shortest. This is all very well for the scientists, but in our everyday lives it's the aesthetic impact that really matters.

Colour is an important part of our daily life and has an influence on the way we live and feel. It is all around us, in nature, in art and decoration, and in the clothes we wear. In nature colour can be used as a signal or warning – red often indicates danger in a poisonous berry or insect – mottled earthy shades provide natural camouflage, and brightly coloured petals attract insects to pollinate a flower.

Colour is an important part of our homes, too. It adds personality and individuality to a room and can also be used to create moods and ambience – to brighten and invigorate or to soothe and calm.

There are trends and fashions in colour which dictate that a certain shade is in vogue or that another is not, but there are also classic colours that can be used at any time. Sometimes it's difficult to know which colour to choose for your home, but if you follow certain guidelines, they will help you use colour with confidence and success.

up close and personal

Choice of colour is a personal thing and people react differently to various colours. For example, some people may find a certain shade of red warm and comforting in a room whereas it makes others feel hot and bothered. This means that when you are choosing colour for a shared or family room, you should either ask other people's opinions or opt for a neutral scheme.

light fantastic

Because light enables us to see colours and since the quality of the light changes with the different seasons and at different times of day, so our perception of how colours look changes too.

colour wheels

The colours of the visible spectrum have traditionally always been illustrated as a colour wheel. This is an important guide to how colours relate to each other and what effect they will have when they are used together.

primaries and secondaries

There are three primary colours – red, yellow and blue – and by mixing these three, the secondary colours are made. When equal amounts of primary colours are blended, for example, red and yellow, then the secondary colour orange is made. Yellow and blue create green and equal parts of blue and red form purple.

10 ideas

tertiaries or hues

The third, or tertiary, range of colours depends on the amount of each colour used. For example, when more yellow than blue is included, the result is a lighter, brighter green, whereas more blue than yellow will produce a darker green. Both these greens are hues of green and both will work well accompanied by the yellow and blue that are adjacent to them on the colour wheel.

harmonies and contrasts

Colours that are next to each other on the colour wheel are referred to as harmonious or family colours and they will be compatible. For example, greens and blues work together because they share a common blue element. Colours that are opposite on the colour wheel, such as red and green, are known as contrasting or complementary colours.

tints

'Tints' are created by the addition of black or white to a colour, for instance, you can add a little or a lot of white to green but in either case the result will be a tint of green.

Black and pure white are not part of the colour spectrum and are, technically, not really colours at all. They are referred to as achromatic colours because they either absorb light, in the case of black, or reflect it, in the case of white, instead of breaking the light down into its component colours. But black and white are important in their own right, especially for decorating, as well as for use in mixing with colours.

tone

'Tone' is used to refer to the intensity (darkness or lightness) of a colour and that is dictated by the amount of black or white present in it. So if a shade of red and a shade of green have the same amount of white in their composition, they will have the same tone.

temperature

The 'temperature' of a colour is dictated by the amount of red or blue in its composition. Red is seen as being a warm colour while blue is classified as cold, so oranges and vibrant pinks – which contain red – are classified as 'hot' colours, whereas turquoise and minty greens are 'cool' because they have blue in their make-up.

balance

Hot and cool colours are frequently used in the same scheme and will balance each other, for example the coolness of blue will cool vibrant orange while the orange will bring warmth to the coolness of the blue.

whites 2

White is one of the oldest decorative colours. Lead pigment was used by the ancient Chinese to give white for their pottery glazes and the Romans favoured white in their clothing and for decoration in their homes. White limewash has traditionally been used to whitewash cottage walls and huts in rural locations around the world and is still popular today for its clean, bright appearance.

Brilliant, or pure, white has a subtle blue hue which can make it a harsh colour to use when you decorate, and although pure white surfaces are good at reflecting light, they can also cause glare. Pure white can also appear cold and stark in grey or dull light. It is often preferable to choose a white that includes a minute element of grey or yellow as this will soften the overall appearance. Some recently developed white paints contain reflective particles which give an even whiter and more brilliant appearance. These can be effective for external paintwork.

a white rule

If you're using white, whether on hard or soft surfaces, you should make sure you keep it well maintained. If a white surface becomes grubby or stained it is instantly noticeable and will make the whole room look shabby. Choose machine-washable white fabrics wherever possible so that you can easily keep them pristine and wipe marks off woodwork as soon as you see them.

neutrals 3

These colours could be defined as 'off-whites' because they are predominantly white but with a quantity of a softening, often warming other colour such as yellow, brown or grey. Popular neutral colours include cream, ivory and buff.

The neutral palette provides a range of useful background colours that are easy to work with and versatile. These soft, classic shades never go out of fashion and can be used in every room in the home. They also work well with strong contrasting colours such as dark browns, black and deep greens.

pastel fact

Pastels form a sub-division of neutrals. These, again, are colours with a high proportion of white but with a definable and specific element of colour, too. Examples of pastel shades are powder blue, rose pink, and butter yellow.

beige beware

Although light, bright and undemanding, a wholly neutral scheme can appear bland and insipid, so neutral colours should be used in moderation and teamed with contrasting or bright colours.

naturals 4

Natural colours are those taken from nature and found in organic materials. In fact, many early colours and dyes were extracted from plants, mineral ores or pigments found in the earth. The colour known as sienna comes from the earth in Tuscany where the pigment was originally found, while charcoal grey was derived from burnt wood.

It is not just plant and earth colours that belong in this category but also the natural materials themselves. Wood ranges from the pale creaminess of sycamore, pine and white elm to the rich chocolate brown and blackness of rosewood, iroko and ebony. Undyed wool varies from cream to pearly grey and dark brown, and stone is similarly diverse, with shades varying from the sandy yellowness of French limestone to the mossy green of Connemara marble.

nature note

Natural colours usually have an intrinsic compatibility because of their earthy origins but they should be used carefully to avoid drabness; too many muddy browns and sludgy greens can be depressing.

5 reds

From the sensual cerise of a long-stemmed rose to the vivid crimson stripe of a patriotic flag, the range of shades that make up the red family are diverse.

Red is said to invigorate the metabolism and the appetite. Perhaps that's why many of its names are associated with food – tomato, raspberry, strawberry and chilli for example.

Red is also the colour of fire and blood, signifies power and has a stimulating effect. It is frequently linked to sensuality too – hence all those bouquets of red roses on Valentine's Day.

Red needs to be treated with care in the home. You should, for example, use it with caution in whole-room schemes, though it is an excellent highlight or accessory colour. If you want to dilute its potency, try teaming it with black, white or cooling blue-based colours.

6 blues

The colour of sky and sea, blue has watery, ethereal connotations. It is regarded as being cool, light and calming and is often used in the decoration of bathrooms and bedrooms. Because it is a colour that signifies cleanliness and spirituality, it has positive overtones and its freshness makes it a frequent choice for the colouring of bath products such as shower gels and lotions which – together with blue-dyed towels – can be used as accessories to bring some colour into a plain white bathroom.

Shades of blue vary from strong cobalt to watery ultramarine, and from greenish prussian to vivid cerulean. In addition many blues are the result of dyeing with indigo and woad – natural pigments which have been used for many centuries.

yellows 7

This is the colour of sunshine, happiness and knowledge, but the richer, more orange tones of yellow can also be used to represent maturity and autumn.

The spectrum of yellow-based colours ranges from acid tones with a citrus or zesty-green base, such as lemon and chrome, to the more muted realms of saffron and mustard. There are also yellows with buttery and cream elements that add a hint of warmth without being overpowering, as well as the earthy hues of ochre. Then there are the colours taken from nature – banana yellow, sunflower, primrose, and buttercup and, with a touch more red, pineapple and orange.

Because of its bright, sunny aspect, yellow is a good colour to use in dark or cold north-facing rooms. If you want to dilute its intensity, add white or use it as a contrast with black and brown. Brown is a sympathetic partner because it contains an element of yellow.

greens 8

Although not a primary colour, green is frequently used in decorating schemes. It combines the spirituality of blue with the emotional warmth of yellow and is a colour that is connected with nature and growth. It is also linked to positive thought and healing – think of the therapeutic benefits of a walk through a leafy wood for clearing your mind and lifting your spirits.

Some of the rich green colours are named after precious stones such as malachite and emerald. Verdigris is a green produced by the elements on copper, another natural substance. Greens such as sage, apple, mint and pea also reflect green's affinity with the natural world.

The soothing and harmonious shades of leafy greens are passive and relaxing and are ideal for living and drawing rooms where you may want to unwind at the end of a busy day. The pale eau de nil and celadon shades, with a high proportion of white in their composition, are lovely greens worth considering for a bedroom scheme.

what colour can do for a room

Whether used in large or small quantities colour will make a significant contribution to any room. The secret is to understand its attributes and to use it in a thoughtful and well-balanced way.

add individuality

If we all lived in identical white boxes life would be very dull and predictable. What colour does is allow us to stamp our individual style and personality on a space, making it our own. Our choice of colours can reflect our interests, culture and character, and may reveal something of our inner self.

enhance

Colour can be used to enhance a room. For example, if the room has an interesting or unusual architectural feature, use colour to highlight it (see 15).

disguise

Colour can also be used to disguise a room's ugly or unbalanced proportions. As a general rule, hot or warm colour will make a wall or object appear to advance, whereas the cool colours will make it recede. You can use this colour rule to help you balance or alter the proportions of a room (see 21).

add light

The judicious use of colour and texture can also help to correct a lack of light. Shiny, metallic surfaces will reflect light (see 33) and pale wall colours will make it feel as if there is more air and space in a room. Simple window dressings that don't impede the light will also help.

be a focal point

Bright cushions on a sofa upholstered in a neutral colour will draw attention to that piece of furniture, as will a vivid rug on a pale wood floor or a vase of bright flowers in otherwise minimal surroundings.

underline a theme

If you opt for a particular decorative theme for a room, whether it's a historic, travel or contemporary theme (see 55, 64 and 72), your choice of colour can be useful in supporting it. For example, red and black are colours that feature in Chinese lacquerwork, so red walls with black gloss woodwork will provide a background against which many oriental fabrics and accessories will look attractive.

Similarly, terracotta is a colour that is associated with Mediterranean countries and when it is used on walls and other surfaces, it is great for enhancing fabrics with bright Mediterranean-style prints and displays of hand-painted ceramics.

In the same way, the more muted palette with a preponderance of greyish blue that is associated with Gustavian and Scandinavian styles sets off accessories and furniture from that period and place.

create a mood

Colour has a psychological effect – each colour has its own energy which can either stimulate or calm. You can use this to create a mood or ambience, for example orange and bright yellow are colours that will invigorate whereas watery blues and greens are said to have a calming, meditative effect.

send a message

Certain colours are associated with cultures, beliefs and symbolism so the use of certain colours in decoration may also impart a message. Red, for example, is linked with radicalism, socialism and revolution, purple is traditionally the colour of royalty, temperance and justice, and in many parts of the world, white denotes purity.

getting to 10
grips with colour

There is really no limit to where you can use colour. It can be applied to virtually any surface in a room – paint, paper, flooring, cushions, furniture, lighting, throws and trimmings. It can be used in moderation for a subtle effect or in volume for maximum impact, but if you are a novice with colour it's best to start with a limited application of neutral or pastel shades. This gives you a chance to become accustomed to its presence and to the effect it has on your surroundings. Then, as you grow used to the subtle palette and gain confidence, you can apply more and stronger colours.

three tips to get you going

1 • soft surfaces

When you're experimenting with colour start with soft furnishings such as cushions and throws. These are easily rearranged and do not require as much money or effort to change as re-painting or re-papering a room.

2 • one wall

Once you're used to the impact of colourful accessories in your room you may want to try a solid panel of colour, for example, painting one wall. Start with a pale colour and then, if you want, you can always increase the strength of colour by adding another coat of a richer hue. Remember that it's easier to apply a darker colour over a lighter one than to obscure a dark colour with a pale one.

3 • try and test

By trying and testing various strengths of colour in different locations around your room you will be able to make a balanced judgement about where the colour looks best, whether you find it more agreeable on smaller or larger surfaces, and if you are ready to embark on a scheme that will embrace the full impact of a bold or bright colour. Designer Donna Karan tests the impact of black on a room by taping up black refuse bags to form a panel so that she can judge its overall affect before committing the area to paint.

colour vogues

Colour trends are fun to follow but should be acknowledged as a passing phase. You can indulge in them by dying voile curtains or throws or changing loose covers on chairs (see 94 and 96), but it can be an expensive commitment to follow colour trends slavishly.

fashion

As interior decoration has become more closely linked with the world of fashion design and designers such as Ralph Lauren, Donna Karan and Missoni have created ranges of homeware and accessories, so palettes of fashion colours for decorating have been developed.

These palettes offer fashionable colour trends that have a seasonal or short-lived shelf life. They are a way of bringing seasonal colour change into our homes just as we make fashion adjustments to our wardrobe. Some items in the home are more susceptible to these fashion changes. For example, bedlinen and towels are not so expensive to replace as carpets and wall coverings; a new set of fashionably coloured and designed duvet covers and pillowcases can bring a fresh new look to the bedroom while a new set of colourful towels can bring a bathroom bang up-to-date.

5 trends

cyclical moods

Colour trends go in cycles; for example, in the 1960s brown, orange and purple were 'trendy' but tastes moved on. Forty years later there was a revival of the sixties look, and these colours became popular again.

evolving trends

Minimalism has had an enormous impact recently. Its trademark colours are white and subtle variations of white, but with the passing of time, minimalism has mellowed and colour is being used to soften the strictness of its purist look (see 73).

technological advances

With advances in technology, new colours and finishes become more widely available or are more commercially viable. Among the recent trends that technology has made possible is the use of metallic, iridescent and fluorescent surface treatments in the home.

nature

Colours that surround us and appear in natural colour combinations are a constant source of inspiration – from the orange petals and green leaves of a marigold to the soft green of pistachio nuts and the yellow, green and red of a ripe apple.

sources of inspiration 12

The question most frequently asked by people embarking on a decorating scheme is 'Where do I start?' In a way it's like answering the first clue in a crossword; once you've established a starting point then the rest will follow, but finding the starting point is the vital key.

baggage

Most people and rooms come with baggage. We all have a few precious belongings, some inherited bits of china or a picture, a comfortable armchair or a table that we can't bear to part with, or a room may come with a fixed feature such as a bathroom suite or a tiled fire surround that you have to work with. Take a long look at what you have got and see if anything about its colour sparks your imagination.

A large piece of furniture such as a sofa or armchair will dominate a room so if it is upholstered in an interesting fabric, you might want to select a colour scheme that complements or contrasts with it. Similarly, if a picture is to be a feature, then you could select a colour that will enhance it – perhaps a dove grey to set off a black frame or a rich red to complement a gilded frame.

history

If your home has any history or period style you may choose to use that as inspiration for a colour scheme and it can be an interesting topic to research. For example, in an apartment in a mid-twentieth-century building you could introduce some furniture from that era by designers Arne Jacobsen or George Nelson, or from manufacturers such as Ercol and Knoll, some of which is still in production today. Much of this furniture is made from moulded plywood which has a warm, rich tone, and the fabrics and colours associated with it are from the strong end of the pastel spectrum. Think Melamine blue, Midwinter or Poole pottery colours, or the dramatic lime green and vivid yellows in the textile prints of Lucienne Day.

magazines and books

These are a good source of ideas. There are many decorating magazines on the newsagent's shelves and they are relatively inexpensive to buy. But don't assume that you'll find your whole scheme pictured in one magazine. What often happens is that you like the floor treatment in one and the wall colour in another. Cut out and collect all the pictures that you like, then spread them on a table to see if they have a common link or if there's a dominant colour in them.

other people's homes

These are an excellent source of ideas, as are show flats and display areas or cameo sets in department stores and furniture shops. In these settings you can see how a colour looks in real life; you can get up close and examine the effect or finish, and in some cases you can even ask for the paint colour reference or the name of the manufacturer. Photographs of these room sets can be a useful reference to take home, but do ask permission before taking a photo in a retail space.

5 ideas

fruit of the imagination

travel

Travel and places you have happy memories of or dream about can also spark ideas, although full-blown fantasy schemes are best saved for private rooms. A memento from a holiday, such as a carpet bought in a souk in Morocco could be your starting point. Use the red, black and white colouring in it to inspire a monochrome scheme of white walls and black-painted floorboards with a highlight colour of red for cushions and the trimming on blinds.

mix and match 13

The colour scheme of a room encompasses many elements, walls, floor, woodwork, soft furnishings, and so on, but they don't all need to be exactly the same colour. In fact, it would be a boring space if they were, so when thinking about a starting colour also view the lighter and darker shades as well as hotter and cooler hues to get a good idea of the variations available.

pick a colour

As a guide, it's best to select just two main colours. Any more and your scheme will begin to look like a random rainbow. Starting with these main colours, you can add lighter and darker shades, or warmer and cooler hues, always aiming for harmony or compatibility between the colours that you choose.

variation on a theme

Pattern and texture are important parts of a colour scheme, and will influence the overall appearance of the room (see 17 and 18), so try to mix plain fabrics with patterned ones and smooth surfaces with quilted or knobbly bouclé finishes, so that there is plenty of variety and interest in the room.

toning down

Remember that even if your walls are destined to be painted in a single strong colour, the impact will be diluted by the mix of furniture, pictures, mirrors and other accessories that will be in the room. All these additional elements will decrease the visible surface area and, if they are in lighter colours, will dilute or lessen the strength of the wall colour.

core collections

A core collection is a range of colours that come from a single main colour that has been mixed and blended to form a wide range of shades and hues. All the colours in the core collection will work together because they share a common base.

how to create a core collection

Think of the core collection as being like a family tree with the main colour as the patriarch and the other colours being the resultant generations. Imagine taupe as the patriarch, used here for the chair and cupboard doors. A large amount of white and some warm yellow is added to a small quantity of the taupe to produce the creamy wall colour. Next a hint of deep red is added to the cream to produce a colour for the curtains that nearly matches the wall colour. More of this same deep red is added to the taupe together with a little of the warm yellow to achieve the rich tawny-brown of the woodwork. Neither the floor tiles nor the rug include the red or yellow but simply rely on the addition of more or less white to create the lighter tints in the taupe spectrum.

You could take this same core collection and extend its range to give you even more colours to use elsewhere in the home. For instance, use the curtain colour as the main colour for your living-room. Add more white to produce a summery pineapple shade for use in a room such as the kitchen. Add either a little black or red, and you will have accent colours to use for accessories (see 15).

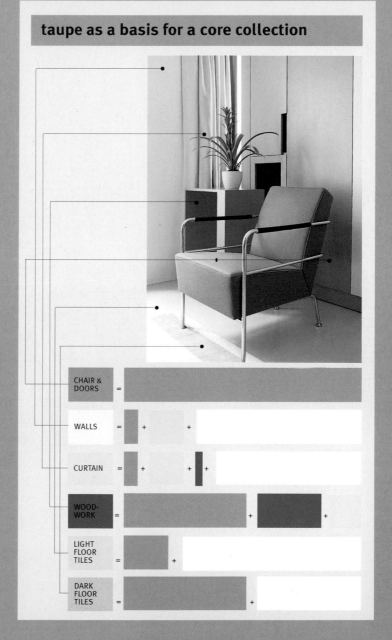

taupe as a basis for a core collection

CHAIR & DOORS	=	
WALLS	=	+	+
CURTAIN	=	+	+	+
WOOD-WORK	=		+	+
LIGHT FLOOR TILES	=		+
DARK FLOOR TILES	=		+

15

accent colour

The most dramatic accent colours are black and white; black makes a bold contrast with white or with the vibrant colours of red, yellow and orange, whereas white will stand out dramatically against navy blue, brown and the darker shades. Accent colours can be used in unexpected places – for instance to highlight the shape of a rug.

opposites attract

Highlight or accent contrasts taken from opposite sides of the colour wheel – for example, red with green or blue with orange – should be used carefully and in moderation otherwise their impact will be lost.

tempered and tonal

Highlight colours don't have to be a dramatic contrast; they can be just a shade or two lighter or darker than the main colour and used subtly, for example to echo or emphasise the shape of a particular feature.

hot metal

Metallics such as gold, silver, copper and brass are useful highlight colours that will lift a dark scheme. Silver's cool tonal links mean it is often used in conjunction with midnight blue, whereas gold, with its element of orange, is compatible with red.

16 quantity and proportion

When you are deciding on a scheme it is important to achieve the right balance of colours and tones. This is difficult to plan on paper because you have to take into consideration the size and placing of objects as well as the effect of lighting and of large single expanses of colour such as on ceilings and floors.

The following guidelines show you one classic way of getting the balance right. Think of your colours as being divided roughly into four. One quarter should be allocated to the first main colour, in this case the yellow of the walls. Allocate another quarter to the second main colour – the white of the woodwork and ceiling – and divide the third quarter between two lighter and darker shades of the main colours, here the grey of the carpet and the beige of the soft furnishings. Divide the final quarter in four – one segment for the two contrasting colours, here the red and blue of the rug, and the other three for the highlight colours of black, gold and brown – the accessories and the wood.

When it comes to choosing your own two main colours, the key to success is achieved by giving one the prime position and the second slightly less emphasis.

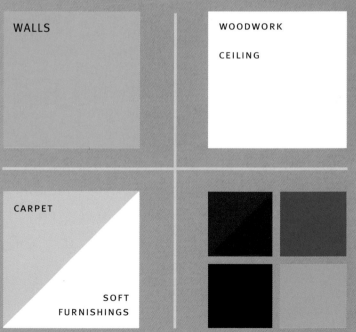

WALLS

WOODWORK

CEILING

CARPET

SOFT FURNISHINGS

colour and pattern 17

Colour and pattern are inextricably linked in decorating schemes, whether it's obvious, as when there's a bold printed fabric or wallpaper, or less apparent, as when pattern in a room is created by the objects that are present. Colour and pattern can combine to bring diverse elements of a scheme together and to unify a space – for example, you can select one or two shades from a patterned wallpaper and use them elsewhere in the room – but take care when using pattern as too much of it can make a space appear cluttered and cramped.

large-scale pattern

When selecting a patterned fabric for curtains or upholstery you should consider the scale of the motif. For example, a large pattern may appear striking when it's used on a scatter cushion but may completely dominate the room on a large piece of furniture or floor-length curtains – though this may be the effect you are looking for. Similarly, broad monochrome deckchair stripes used horizontally on a rounded, well-stuffed armchair will exaggerate its size and make it look unwieldy.

small-scale pattern

A sea of tiny sprigs and miniature floral prints can look bitty and insignificant in a room. To prevent this from happening, try to use a balanced mix of patterned and single-colour surfaces. The plain elements will help counteract the busy-ness of the pattern and the single colours can be chosen so that they underline the main shades used in the print.

hardly-there pattern

Patterns and designs can play tricks on the eye. For example, many colours in an intricate pattern may appear to blend together and, from a distance, look like one overall colour, but close up you will see that there is a variety of shades in a pattern consisting of many individual shapes. When you are trying to colour-match a material or paper with this type of composition, you should pick out just one of its individual colours.

colour, pattern and history

Certain patterns, colours and styles of weave and print, are appropriate to certain periods and styles of décor. For example, a sweeping, two-tone burgundy, figured damask curtain would look out of place in a modern minimalist setting but would be perfectly at home in a mid-nineteenth-century room.

made to match

Many fabric and wallpaper sample books include patterns that are designed to be used together. In general these will consist of a floral or more complex pattern with a simple or geometric co-ordinating design. Mixing patterns can be very effective and can add another layer of interest to a scheme.

Using ranges that are designed to go together can help you achieve a good result if you're not confident in your own ability to mix and match.

pairs and positions

The arrangement of furniture and accessories in a room creates its own patterns. These patterns also play their part in a decorative scheme, but it is an idea that can be difficult to grasp. For example, a pair of matching chairs placed either side of a window will create a simple pattern based on parallel lines – the vertical and horizontal lines of the window frame and of the chairs – while a group of framed pictures on a wall will form either squares or rectangles. Pairs of objects have a symmetry which the eye always finds pleasing.

colour and texture 18

Surfaces and finishes have inherent texture that affects the play of light and so influences how colour is perceived.

two-tone

In shot silk the weft thread is one colour and the warp another. When you view the fabric straight on it appears to be a blend of the two colours, but seen from one direction one colour is dominant and from the other the other is stronger.

mixed surfaces

The weave of fabrics such as jacquard appears lighter in some areas and darker in others. The smoother areas reflect the light and so appear lighter while the matt areas absorb the light and appear darker.

matt, flat and irregular

Pile and surface irregularities also cause light to refract and reflect in different ways, so a sisal-weave floor covering may be made from a uniform colour, but its ribbing actually gives it lines of light and shade.

gloss or no gloss

A deep indigo ceramic tile with a high-glaze finish will look dark blue but because its surface is smooth and shiny, it will reflect light and seem less solid and dense, whereas wool felt in the same colour absorbs the light and so appears flatter and darker.

the perfect finish

If you decide to use slate or some other natural stone as a worktop or floor covering, you will have a choice of finishes. If you leave the surface plain it will have a matt appearance, or you can seal it with a matt varnish, in which case it will become slightly darker and will have a very slight sheen. If you oil its surface, slate will become noticeably darker and have a more marked lustre.

three practical pointers

1 • Pale-coloured, deep-textured fabrics aren't a practical choice for fixed upholstery in a home where young children and animals live, because the surface will quickly and easily become marked. It is much better to choose a dark colour and a flat weave. These are more forgiving and resilient for this type of situation.

2 • Dark-coloured thick, chunky, open-weave tweeds or stiff glazed cottons in rich, deep shades will neither fold easily nor reflect the light so if they are used for curtains they are unlikely either to sit well or to enhance a narrow window that does not let in much light.

3 • Lightweight pale-coloured gauzes or fine silk fabrics do not work as chair upholstery. They do not cover satisfactorily nor do they withstand everyday wear and tear sufficiently well.

using a swatch board 19

The best way to work out your palette of colours is to create a swatch board. This will allow you to get an overall impression of how the various elements of your scheme will work together. All you need is a large sheet of hardboard and some glue, staples or drawing pins. If your board isn't white, cover it with a sheet of wallpaper lining paper or plain white paper to give a neutral and consistent background.

Glue swatches or samples of the floor covering onto the board, then add small squares of the paint colours you are considering, followed by fabric swatches for upholstery, curtain materials and trimmings until you have all the elements from each part of the room.

Once you have assembled the board you can gauge how the various elements of your scheme are coming together, and then ask yourself, does this palette look a bit too similar and bland? If so, what else do I need?

four questions and answers to help you decide

1 • Would a highlight colour help? Choose a highlight colour from the opposite side of the colour wheel from your main colour. This opposite, or contrasting, colour will bring the touch of excitement and vigour to your scheme that it needs.

2 • Are the colours all the same tone? If they are, that may be making the scheme bland. Darker and lighter shades add richness; think of them as shadows and accents.

3 • Is it all looking a bit smooth and samey? Variations in pattern and texture will add interest (see 17 and 18); include a few tapestry or woven tweed cushions and throws amongst the soft plain wool ones.

4 • Do I lack defining accessories? Would the glitter of silver, glass or gold, or the earthy warmth of wood or stone help to lift my colours?

20 colour to enhance

Colour is a useful tool to highlight one or more features in a room.

accentuate

You could accentuate the recess of a graceful niche and make a
dramatic statement by painting it in a contrasting colour to the rest of
the room, or for an understated effect, choose a darker or lighter tone of
the main wall colour.

create a frame

Standard features in a
room such as door and
window frames and
skirting boards are
usually painted in white
gloss and act as a frame to the wall and ceiling
or the window, but to make more of these features and enhance the
overall impact of the room you can paint the woodwork in a different
colour. For example, gloss woodwork in rich brown with the wall and
skirting board in a soft mink colour butting up against a beige carpet
looks extremely effective as does black gloss woodwork with walls
painted in flannel grey and teamed with a deep plum carpet.

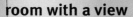

room with a view

Colour can be used to enhance a view from a room. If you have French
windows that look out over a garden with lush lawns and hedges, then
a hint of green in your room's colour scheme will help to link the indoor
and outdoor spaces. If your view is of sky and sea or of a river bank,
then elements of blue – maybe a couple of cushions and a rug, teamed
with shiny glass vases and a large mirror –
will help to echo the vista.

gently does it

Natural colours, such as the
warm wood tones of old furniture
or well-worn parquet flooring will
appear more mellow if they are
next to a neutral or off-white wall
and skirting board rather than
next to pure white. The hint of
colour means there is less of a
dramatic contrast and the effect
will be more flattering.

21
colour to conceal

Colour can be used to conceal less desirable features of a room so if, for instance, your room is very small, choose a cool colour, such as one with a blue hue. Since cool colours tend to recede (see 9), the walls will appear to fade into the distance rather than hem you in. Conversely, warm, dark colours, such as those with a reddish hue give a sense of enclosure, so if a room has a ceiling that is too high, painting it a rich, dark reddish-brown will make it feel lower. Similarly, if a room feels too open and uninviting, a rich, dark colour on one or more walls will make it more intimate.

If you have an unattractive or bulky piece of furniture in a room, such as an unattractive wardrobe you've inherited or an over-large sofa, paint the wardrobe or cover the sofa with a throw in a plain, subtle colour. This will have the effect of making the furniture appear less obvious.

Or use bright colour – maybe with pattern – to divert the eye from an unattractive feature. For example, a strategically placed vivid hanging can divert the attention from an ugly view through the window or away from a less-than-perfect wall surface

22
which colour where?

Some colours are used more frequently in certain areas of the home than others. Sometimes this is a fashionable trend but it may be for practical reasons.

use this here

• Blue is a colour that's associated with water and is therefore often used for tiles and paintwork in 'watery' rooms such as bathrooms.

• White is regarded as clean and pure, so is ideal for a kitchen. In modern homes, though, the kitchen tends to be more of a family room, so the white needs to be warmed up and made less clinical. This can be done either by injecting some contrast colour into the room or by mixing a colour into the white to give a pastel or natural shade.

• Yellow is regarded as a happy, sunny colour and it suits most rooms in the house, but pick the shade of yellow carefully so that it isn't too 'hot' or dominant and always use it in conjunction with a second colour.

don't use this there

• Grey is rarely found in a kitchen because sludgy greys can look grubby and that is inappropriate for a room where cleanliness is important. High-gloss grey cabinet doors are sometimes found in cutting-edge kitchens, but the grey often has a light or white base and its effect is frequently diluted by the use of white walls, worktops or tiles.

• Black is seldom used as a major decorative colour. A wholly black room would be dark and funereal. Limit your use of black to highlights or furniture.

take care with these anywhere

• Red is a colour that needs to be treated with great care in any decorative scheme. Bright or pillar-box red is often associated with passion and may be used in a bedroom, but many people regard red as the colour of anger and danger so they prefer not to use it in any room where they want to relax.

• Cool blues and colours with white or grey tints can make you feel cold and isolated. Opt instead for colours with a hint of red, such as hyacinth blue or bluebell, as these have a softer, warmer appearance.

colour and daylight

23

Before you commit to any colour or apply it in a room, it's important to view it in a variety of different lights to gauge how it reacts. Natural light, or daylight, is not only a free source of illumination but shows colours at their truest.

You may also select colours to work with the available light in your room. For example, if you have a north-facing room that gets little direct daylight and so feels cold, then a warm colour – one with some red or yellow in it – will help to make the room feel more hospitable. Conversely, a very warm and sunny room can be made to feel more comfortable if painted in a cool shade, for example, fresh minty green, turquoise or a shade of blue.

24 rooms with too much light

On bright days sunlight can cause glare and intense sunshine will bleach fabrics as well as cause the ambient temperature to rise.

three tips for feeling cool

1 • The best way of regulating the flow of sunshine is with blinds and shutters; they can be adjusted and manoeuvred throughout the course of the day. When you close the shutters the colours in the room will appear darker and more sombre and this will help you to feel cooler too.

2 • Avoid colours with a lot of white in their composition; these light, bright colours reflect the light and the heat of the sun and may cause glare as well.Think of Mediterranean countries, where people often dress in light-absorbing black, and opt for darker or cooler colours instead.

3 • Cool colours, for instance those with a blue base, help to make a room feel less hot and dazzling. Turquoise is an especially useful colour for an over-bright room as it combines the freshness of green with the wateriness of blue. Avoid the red, bright yellow and strong orange colour ranges as these are hot and will exaggerate the feeling of heat in the room.

colour and artificial light

Colours may look different in artificial light compared with daylight. For example, yellow paintwork can appear rich and golden in natural light, but in artificial illumination, say low-voltage halogen, which is often used for recessed ceiling lights, it may take on a green hue which gives a sludgy, muted appearance.

As well as viewing paint colours in different types of artificial light you will also need to check fabric swatches to make sure that they not only work well with your choice of paint, but also that they retain their colour.

six artificial light sources

1 • Full-spectrum lights. These give a clear white light. They can be useful in a dark room during daylight hours, but can be a bit soulless and harsh in the evening. As this light mimics daylight, colours will appear the same as in natural illumination.

2 • Halogen lights. Whether these are mains-voltage or low-voltage, they will emit a bright white light, but if connected to a dimmer, the level of light can be lowered or raised to a comfortable and flattering level. At full strength this light may reduce the impact of a strong colour but at a lower level it should have little effect on colour intensity.

3 • Tungsten bulbs. These give a soft, yellowish light and are the most commonly used in general household lighting. Their yellow hue can enhance the richness of yellow but may make blues appear green and whites, off-white.

4 • Fibre-optic lighting. This is increasingly found in modern domestic settings. It gives a clean white light which can appear to bleach or whiten colours close to it.

5 • Fluorescent lights. These usually come in strips and give off a cold, flat light that is not very flattering to rich colours or fabrics. They are usually used for work areas, for example, fitted to the bottom of kitchen wall units to illuminate the work surface below.

6 • Candles. These produce a warm, flattering yellow glow that is relaxing and calming. They may be used in conjunction with a low-level electric light which can lessen the orange intensity of the flame. They will enhance rich colours such as red, orange and gold but may 'yellow' or taint white and off-white tones.

lampshades, lamps and colour

26

There's a huge choice of lampshades available to suit every style of room but you need to bear in mind that each one will subtly alter the colour you see.

• A metal cone will direct the light upwards and downwards but does not allow it to penetrate its sides. This means that colour on walls and ceiling directly above and below the cone will be fully lit and bright, but the rest of the room will appear to be in a darker colour or less intense shade.

• Coloured fabric or coloured glass shades will direct the beam but will allow a certain amount of light to glow through the shade. For example, if the shade has a rich red covering or is made of red glass, the light that comes through it will have a reddish hue, which will, in turn, impart a reddish cast to the other colours in the room.

• Light passing through pale cream fabric, plain white paper or opaque glass shades will become diffuse and softer but will not have any impact on the colours used in the decoration of the room.

• A shade with a metallic silver inner surface will reflect a cool, white light, whereas a gold inner surface will give a mellow yellow hue. The reflected light from the silvered shade will not affect other colours nearby but the gold may add a small amount of yellow hue to the colours immediately adjacent to it.

try and test

When buying a lampshade it is worth taking along your paint samples and fabrics swatches on a piece of board. That way you can see how they will appear in the artificial light and what influence the colour of the shade will have on them.

spaces without natural light 27

Hallways, bathrooms, cloakrooms and lavatories are often windowless and so require careful colour planning to prevent them from being dark, uninviting, boxy spaces.

One way to create an impression of space and light in a windowless space is to use reflective surfaces like mirror (see 28), glass, metals such as stainless steel (see 33) or resin, lacquer and high-gloss finishes (see 31). In a small cloakroom or separate lavatory, for example, you could fill one whole wall with mirror and balance the mirror with dark rich tones by using deep plum suede-effect wallpaper or dark blue towels. This can be extremely dramatic.

You should treat main bathrooms that lack natural light differently though. Here you will be getting ready first thing in the morning and perhaps unwinding and relaxing in a bath in the evening, so you will need a colour scheme and lighting that are adaptable and can easily take you from one mood to another.

Hallways with little or no natural light are especially problematic (see 54). A hallway should be welcoming and, as it leads you from the front door through to the other rooms, it also needs to be light. Here again, use mirrors if you can to enhance the sense of space and bolster the effect by using light, bright colours.

28

it's all done with mirrors

Just as a metallic inner surface of a lampshade reflects light, so will a mirror, but a mirror will also double the effect of any illumination. This means that in daylight the brightness of a room will be increased and the colours in it will appear sharper. It also means that in artificial light, the yellowness of any tungsten light or of candles placed in front of the mirror will be doubled – resulting in an increased yellow hue.

29 colour in small rooms

Small rooms are best decorated in pale or light colours to give a feeling of space and brightness; colours from the white (see 2), neutral or pastel (see 3) and natural colour ranges (see 4) are a good place to start.

But small rooms don't need to be dull. Use bright accessories to add character and colour and, wherever possible, keep window treatments simple so that the view and daylight are unhindered.

As in windowless rooms, mirror and other reflective surfaces are useful to add to the illusion of space. A mirror could, for example, echo the view from a window or reveal a corridor beyond the room. Mirror will also have the effect of echoing and doubling the impact of any colour you add to your scheme so if you are also using accessories in rich or dark colours, select them carefully to ensure that they do not overwhelm the room's limited amount of space.

Storage is essential to small spaces; if things are tidily stowed, the room will immediately appear more capacious. And cupboard doors that are painted to match the walls will blend in and become almost unnoticeable.

Finally, keep the colour scheme simple – a main colour for walls and floor and just one or two contrast colours for furniture and accessories.

colour in big rooms

30

Large rooms, especially those with generously proportioned windows, can accommodate rich, dark colours with ease. If you use pale, white-based hues or pure white, you run the risk of making the room appear even bigger, cold and more empty.

For large expanses of plain wall, try mixing and matching colours rather than using one single colour on all four walls. For example, paint two opposite walls in a rich aubergine and the other two in a luxurious cream. Or, if the room is uncomfortably high-ceilinged, draw the attention to its width by painting the walls in horizontal stripes in a palette of harmonious shades as seen here. These colours vary from a matt reddish-brown through to a high-gloss chocolate. The variation in the paint finishes helps add interest to the visual effect.

31 glossy colour

There are a number of finishes that you can either apply to a surface to give it a high gloss, or that are inherently glossy themselves. The result is one of richness, opulence, and often drama. Whichever gloss you choose, remember that bright colours with a shiny surface will seem more vivid and dark and will appear to have more depth and richness, so you should be careful how you use them. Large areas of a glossy colour can be overwhelming, so be sure to temper them with plenty of matt surfaces and lots of texture in the shape of curtain and upholstery fabrics, cushions, throws, rugs and other floor coverings.

glossy paint

The most common and relatively unobtrusive high-gloss finish is achieved by using gloss paint. This is usually found on woodwork, skirting boards, doors and window frames because of its resilience to withstand knocks, but it can also be used on walls to achieve a finish similar to lacquer. Acrylic paint is another glossy option. This has a shiny, almost plasticised, finish and comes in a wide range of colours.

glossy finishes

When it comes to applied glossy finishes, choose from lacquer, varnishes, glazes or waxes.
• Lacquer is a coloured varnish of shellac diluted with alcohol and is traditionally applied in several coats, each of which is sanded until perfectly smooth. It imbues surfaces with a very smart, elegant finish.

• Varnishes, whether polyurethane or acrylic, can be clear or coloured and may be applied layer on layer to achieve a really hard, high gloss.
• Glazes can be used in various ways – to give a slight sheen and linear textural effect or a broken, crazed surface.
• Waxes create a glossy surface, especially on good quality woods. A rich lustrous appearance can be achieved on furniture, doors and floors by applying beeswax, while coloured waxes can be used to intensify the colour of natural wood or to stain or tint pale woods as well as to add a sheen.
• Polyurethane coatings and synthetic polymer blends can be used to achieve a hardwearing high sheen on the fronts of kitchen units and on wardrobe or cupboard fronts.

32

matt and flat colour

Colour that is matt and flat absorbs light so it will look softer than colour with a shinier surface. Matt colour has a comforting, mellow, easy-to-live with appearance that suits most styles of decoration but especially traditional styles and period looks – particularly since many shiny surfaces are more recent inventions.

matt paint

Matt paints include distemper, limewash or whitewash, flat oil and matt emulsion.

• Distemper is an old, chalky traditional wall and ceiling paint that has recently undergone a revival and is now available in a range of colours that look soft, faded and almost frosted. It especially suits rustic styles of interiors. As it is a chalk- and water-based product it is ecologically sound but should be applied directly to a freshly plastered surface. It isn't waterproof so is not recommended for use in bathrooms or kitchens and it cannot be painted over with any other type of paint. If you want a change, you have to wash it off first.
• Limewash or whitewash is another wall paint, for use inside or outside. It is made from slaked lime and water and can be coloured with pigments. It dries to an attractive matt finish but its main disadvantage is its soft surface which may leave a powdery residue on anything that brushes against it.
• Flat oil paint is an oil-based paint that, like distemper, has undergone a revival recently. It provides a very durable finish that is used for woodwork wherever a fine, smooth, matt surface is required.
• Matt emulsion offers a contemporary solution for walls and ceilings. It is inexpensive, has a soft, non-shiny appearance and dries to a firm set but it lacks something of the chalkiness of the old-fashioned preparations.

matt fabrics

Many fabrics have a matt finish but especially those made with natural fibres, for example cotton muslin, linen, worsted wool, flannel and towelling. These fabrics are versatile enough to suit any style of decoration and are especially effective when they are contrasted with shinier surfaces.

glossy fabrics

There are also gloss fabrics such as plastic-coated PVC and highly finished leather, but these surfaces can be slippery and uncomfortable to sit on. The most popular glossy surface furnishing material is chintz; a glazed or mercerised cotton which comes in single colours or floral prints. Satin or satinised fabrics, silk velvet and fur also have a surface sheen which makes them ideal for glamorous and opulent decorating schemes.

metals and metallics 33

Metals and metallic colours add glitter and richness to all decorative schemes whether the finish has a high shine or is matt and muted. You can go for the metal itself in some form – objects made from metal, metallic thread, metal leaf – or for metallic paints, powders and glazes, and you can use metals and metallics either in large amounts to make a dramatic statement or to pick out some detail – an architrave or picture frame for instance.

the real thing

Metal in its own right has become a mainstay of kitchen design with pre-formed stainless-steel surfaces, splashbacks, extractor hoods and ovens now commonplace. The bathroom is a room where metals are essential as well as popular, with chrome taps, steel bowls and basins and even double-skin steel baths. In either kitchens or bathrooms, teaming the metal with glass gives a cool, hi-tech, modern look, but this can be softened if you wish by adding a natural material such as wood which will also bring a suggestion of colour to the room.

Metals can easily be introduced into other rooms, for example a burnished brass table, a pair of gleaming silver candlesticks, a glistening copper dish, a brass lampholder, or they can appear in the form of fabrics embellished with gold or silver threads woven into the cloth or applied as embroidery to the surface.

Then there's gold and silver leaf which can turn any mundane surface into a glittering prize. They have been used for centuries to gild decorative objects such as picture frames and overmantels, but there is now a fashion for using them as a decorative wall feature. Laid side by side and brushed into position gold or silver leaf will form a panel of small reflective squares which will change in appearance according to the direction of the light and its source. A silver-leaf wall will look cool and blue in daylight, but in candlelight it will take on a warm golden hue. But be warned, it doesn't come cheap.

a hint of metal

If you don't want the metal itself but still want to create a bold impression, then look at the range of wallpapers with metallic finishes that are available. You may not want to paper a whole room with one of these, but they make a dramatic statement on a single wall or in an alcove. And they're also good for bringing light into a windowless space or one where there isn't much natural light (see 27).

Smaller touches of metallic colour can be provided by metallic glazes, paints and powders. These can either be the colour of the metal itself, or can combine a metallic appearance with a colour such as blue or green. The finished surface has a hard but glittering appearance, like that of car body paint. Metallic glazes and finishes can also be found on ceramics, either all over or to give a shining rim or motif on a plate or bowl. Metallic-coloured paints and powders are best used in moderation for features such as a table top, a door frame or a fire surround; too much of them may make a room look overly glitzy and shiny.

use a base coat

An effective way of using a metallic finish is to apply it over a coloured base. For example, if you want a plain silver appearance, apply silver leaf or paint over a white or pale grey undercoat. Alternatively, you can achieve a delicate effect by applying bronze powder over a pastel-pink painted wall with a stippling brush or sponge. The result will be a hint of the bronze rather than a solid mass. These finishes can be effective in a room with limited natural light as the reflectiveness of the metallic finish will amplify what light is available.

34
iridescent and pearlised colours

Iridescent colours appear to be made up of many colours and as you look at them, the colours appear to change. Iridescent paints, glass, and fabrics such as voile and plasticised materials, can also have a pearlised finish which gives them a white lustre as well as adding elements of yellow, pink, blue and purple.

Iridescent colours are effective in a bathroom because of their shimmery, watery appearance. They also suit bedrooms where they can add a soft, restful and beautiful ethereal quality.

colour to suit the mood

Think about colour and mood in the context of fashion and that will help you see how, on a larger scale and used in a room scheme, colour will have a similar effect. For example, if you wear a charcoal grey outfit it makes you look more sombre and puts you in a more sober mood than if you wore the same outfit in a vibrant pillar-box red or shocking pink. This shows you how colour has a way of affecting the mind and body.

hedge your bets

You can vary the mood in a single room by choosing a main colour that combines two elements, for example purple, which is made up of hot, vibrant red and cool, calming blue. Whenever you want to feel cool and calm, increase the amount of blue in the room by adding some blue accessories – a blue vase and a throw, for example. When you want to enhance the vibrant feel, add red flowers, a bowl of red apples and some red cushions.

light and shade

Lighting is an important part of creating a mood (see 25). As well as having a task light for working, have a variety of levels of lighting in a room, preferably on dimmer switches. When you want to unwind you can dim the lights to create a more restful mood. Remember though that low light reduces the intensity of all colours so may reduce dark shades to a dull and uniform blackness.

colour and scent

Mood, colour and scent are all linked so pleasing the olfactory as well as the visual sense will add to your feelings of wellbeing. For example, purple is a calming, cleansing colour, and is also the colour of lavender flowers which have a soothing, relaxing aroma. Yellow is an uplifting colour and is often associated with the scent of zesty lemon, which will awaken the senses and invigorate the mind.

find a focus

Set aside different parts of a room to be a focus for various moods and activities and link a certain colour to them. For example, a green chair and footstool by the window to relax and watch the sky and trees; an armchair with a blue cushion near the CD player to listen to music and stimulate the auditory senses; an area with a rich brown, earthy and grounding wooden table and some task lighting to make reading and working a pleasure. Occasionally leave the room and go outdoors for a vigorous walk and take in the wide variety of colours in the landscape. When you come back, the colours and aspect of your room will appear fresh and inviting.

eastern promise

The Chinese believe that the elements play an important part in creating mood and wellbeing. Their five elements are: Earth – brown, yellow and orange, promoting wholeness and unity; Metal – gold, silver and white, representing children and leadership; Water – blue, purple and black for career, power and knowledge; Wood – green for family, health and life; and Fire – red, for passion, wealth and money.

accessory after the fact

The mood of a room can be altered by the colour of the accessories you put with it. For example, a room that is predominantly red will appear more exciting and stimulating if you add orange and yellow accessories whereas adding black accessories will calm and relax the mood.

with feeling

The sense of touch is acute so texture combined with colour can also influence mood and emotion. For example, think of the difference between the cool, white crispness of freshly laundered linen and the soft sensuousness of a midnight-blue, silk velvet. When dressing a room, take texture and touch into consideration as well as colour.

flower power

Flowers and plants bring colour to a room and sometimes that colour changes as the days pass, bringing a change of colour emphasis. A bowl of daffodil bulbs starts as predominantly green and then the flowers bloom and bring a splash of yellow to the room. A bunch of almond-blossom twigs start out brown, then burst into pale pink blossom.

beat the blues

If you're in a bad mood, feeling under the weather or depressed, think of white space. Try and clear clutter away from your home, tidy the surfaces and visualise moving from a black or grey atmosphere into a pure, white clean space.

moving on

Once you've got rid of your black or grey mood and mentally achieved your white space, take the next step. Bring some fresh, bright colour into your room and rearrange your furnishings and accessories. That way the colour emphasis will be different and it will feel as though you've created a fresh new space.

10 ideas

36
restful colour

Restful colours are useful as a background in areas such as living rooms, bedrooms and bathrooms. Neutrals such as ivory and buff, mushroom and magnolia are calming, uncomplicated colours that suit these rooms They demand little of us visually but provide a soft, slightly warm background against which any other colour can be placed. Their undemanding presence also makes them universal; they can be used for virtually any theme or style of decoration.

Certain shades of grey may also be classed as neutrals but they should be chosen with care if you want them to feel calming. Select a light, clean shade, for example, a pearl grey or stone rather than a dark, oppressive charcoal or a grubby grey with green or yellow undertones.

Apart from their soft visual presence, neutral colours also have connections with nature and familiar things, so we tend to associate these

colours with pleasant memories and that makes us feel calm. Many of the neutrals are named after the raw materials they are similar to, for example, driftwood, cream, ivory, straw, sandstone and biscuit.

There are also other subtle, elegant and more colour-defined shades that have a calming, restful effect. For example, pale blue can be serene and inspiring and those shades of purple that include an element of dusky grey – lilac and pink for example – are also restful and soothing.

Certain shades of green can also feel calming and cool. A green room is traditionally where actors meet and relax before they go on stage. Green was also often used to paint hospital walls in order to help patients feel less nervous about their treatment. But it's important to get the right shade; if the green is too vivid, it can have the opposite effect and make you feel overly invigorated and alert.

37

invigorating colour

The primary colours are bright and cheerful and are useful for kitchens, play areas and family rooms, but they should be treated with caution because too much of any of them can be over-stimulating.

the primaries

Yellow is invigorating and is also regarded as a happy colour; it raises the spirits and brings a sense of joy. It is reminiscent of sunny days and is the colour of sunflowers, daffodils and primroses. But yellow is a notoriously difficult

colour to decorate with. It is one of the most changeable colours in different lights, so do trials and test patches (see 40) before you commit to buying a yellow-based fabric or paint.

Red is another lively colour. It is full of vitality, drama and energy and is regarded as the most powerful colour of all. It can be hot and brilliant, as in scarlet and poppy, or spicy with a touch of brown or orange, like paprika or chilli. But add some blue to red and the red cools and is no longer energising.

The other primary colour, blue, can be exhilarating but it needs to be a punchy electric blue, turquoise or similarly vibrant shade with touches of yellow (think of yellow's sunny disposition). Avoid too much red with blue as red can then merge into purple hues which are more comtemplative and meditative.

the secondaries

Secondary colours that use yellow as a base inherit its uplifting aspect. For example, acidic lime green and vibrant tangerine have a large proportion of yellow in their make-up and are both zesty and invigorating. Vibrant greens such as grass, apple and mint are shades that represent growth and freshness; they revitalise and stimulate, too.

and don't forget white

Pure white is fresh, clean, cool and bright and feels stimulating if it is well lit. As a background, it will enhance bright colours set against it, but too much white on its own can be negative, giving a feeling of isolation and low energy.

38
thoughtful colour

Colours that make us feel thoughtful are suitable for work spaces, studies, private sitting rooms and, in some cases, bedrooms, but that depends on your character and preferences. Thoughtful, contemplative shades revolve around the mid-tones – so not as pale as the neutrals or as strong as full colour. They may have elements of both white and black in their make-up and sometimes a soft almost dusty quality.

Green is acknowledged for its cooling and calming effect, but certain soft shades of green such as celadon, sage and jade can also impart a meditative aura. These soft shades also marry well with natural wood such as ash, elm or oak and can be used to create an understated and uncomplicated scheme for a room where you might want to work or simply be calm and relaxed.

Blue, especially the slightly warmer tones of blue that contain a hint of pink or lavender, can invigorate the mind and warm up the thought processes. In the yellower, turquoise tones, blue is also known for its beneficial meditative, mind-clearing and inspirational effects.

39

sociable colour

Whether it's your family sitting room, a room where friends gather, or a work space where you mix with your colleagues, the choice of colour can help to set the right mood.

Pale yellow is a sociable and gregarious colour; it has a sunny, warming and happy effect on people and if used in white-based tints, it also appears fresh and cleansing.

Rust and terracotta and the more muted shades of the orange family also feel warm, friendly and sociable. But they are red-based colours which can be hot and angry, so they should be tempered with calming and neutralising shades such as navy blue, sienna brown or black, which will bring balance and calm to the scheme.

dos and don'ts

do aim for the majority of the scheme in a social area to be in subtle colours with white to bring freshness and light.

don't use classic gender colours such as pink and blue as they can often be thought stereotypical or child-like.

do keep the floor areas clean and uncluttered and use a darker grounding shade to give the room a feeling of stability and base.

don't overload with colourful accessories as these can be distracting and cluttering.

get practical: paint trials and tests

Trials and test patches are a must when colour-scheming, not just to ensure that the colour is as you expect in various lights, but also to check that fabrics are compatible with paints and flooring as well as with upholstery and furniture. The best way to test paint is to try it out on a piece of white board or a length of lining paper. The board or paper have the advantage of being moveable so you can pin or tape them to various parts of the wall. And if you use a length of lining paper, you can test-paint a much larger area, which will give you a better idea of how the colour will appear in volume.

three helpful hints to get the colour right

1 • First, pin or tape the painted board or paper to the wall by the window. Look at the colour in full natural light and at different times of the day – morning, noon and dusk. Then, since shadow can make some colours appear gloomy, move the sample to a dark corner of the room, and repeat the experiment.

2 • Check the colour in different types of artificial light.

3 • Check your main colour against the other colours in your scheme. If you put a strong red curtain next to a cold blue wall in a room with a cool northerly light, the contrast might be too dramatic, but if you change the wall colour to a shade of blue with a warm, pinkish undertone it will help balance it with the colour of the curtain.

extend your options

When trying a test patch of colour it is worth getting two or three different shades. For example, if you are choosing a blue, try a 'control' or standard blue as well as one that has more red and another that has more yellow. This will help focus your mind and eye.

get practical: undercover story

Background or undercoat colours, whether in paint, fabric or other finishes will affect the appearance of any colour you put on top.

curtains and blinds

If you want to line curtains or a blind made from a light floral print, a white or off-white lining will enhance the floral's delicate appearance. Save dark linings for richly coloured and textural fabrics such as velvet, chenille and jacquard. If you require darkness at bedtime, use black-out blinds or curtains that you only draw at night.

paint procedure

Be sure to choose the correct colour undercoat when painting. If the wall or paintwork is dark and you want to paint a lighter colour on top then the undercoat you use should be white or pale to obliterate the existing colour. If you paint your pale colour directly onto the darker colour, the original colour will show through and your new colour will come up too dark. Check with your paint or DIY shop to get the correct base colour so that your chosen colour will appear as you want it.

42

get practical: durability and fade factor

Most modern fabrics and paints are chemically configured to be durable and fade-resistant but bright sunshine can cause richly coloured fabrics, carpets and throws to fade. This isn't necessarily a bad thing as faded kelims and dhurries can take on an interesting and attractive aged appearance, but in general it is not desirable. To guard against fading, use voile curtains or venetian blinds to exclude or diminish the effect of sunlight in a room.

top tips

• Curtains that fade at the leading edge can be swapped around annually so that the edge where the colour is most affected by the sun becomes the outer edge, and vice versa.

• Certain paint finishes such as limewash and distemper have a chalky surface which can brush off on people's clothing, leaving a powdery white film (see 32). Such paints are also absorbent and so are more likely to be discoloured by oil marks and greasy fingers. If you are using these finishes on walls, and especially if they are in white or a pale colour, you might consider protecting them (and people's clothes) with a dado rail.

43

get practical: the right order

When you are decorating, always work in the correct order. That way you keep dust to a minimum and protect floors, fabrics and upholstery from wet paint, glues and varnishes.

1 • Apply the ceiling and wall colour before starting on the gloss or woodwork.

2 • Put the flooring in before you start arranging the fabrics.

3 • Add the furniture and accessories when all the surfaces are dry, the flooring has been finished and the curtains have been hung.

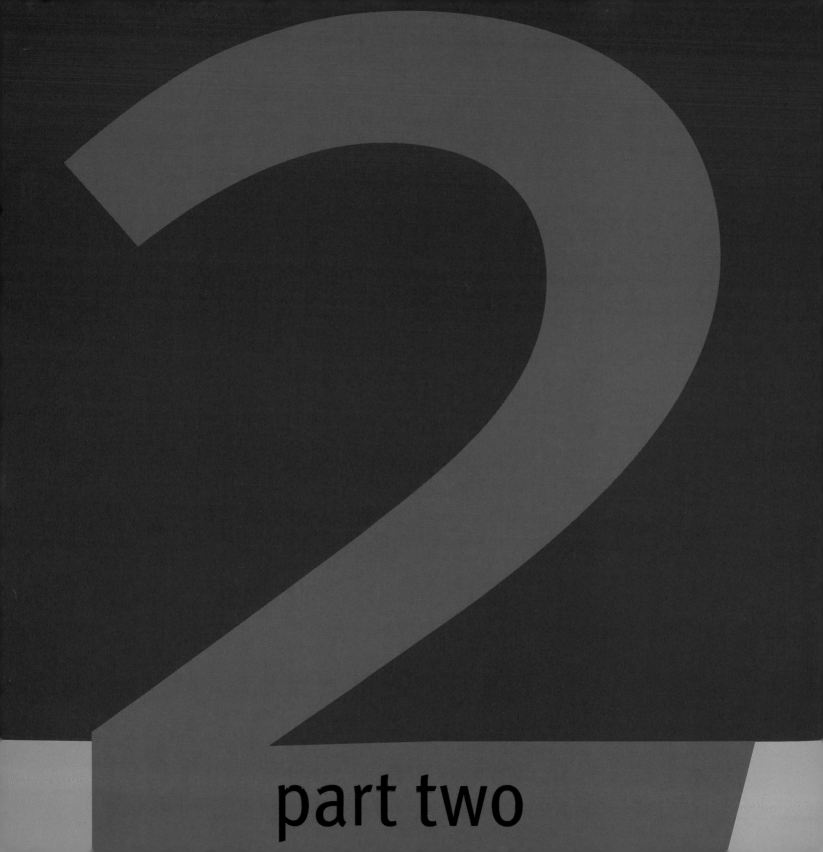

part two

getting down to the detail

44 colour and space

When creating a decorating scheme always bear in mind the interplay between colour, light and space. All three of these elements are part of the whole equation.

forwards and backwards

Just as warm colours advance and cool colours recede (see 9), so dark shades tend to advance and pale ones recede. Apply this knowledge to a room, using cool, pale shades to give a sense of greater space and warm dark shades for a greater sense of enclosure.

focal points and space

When your eye is attracted to a windowbox of vivid yellow daffodils outside a grey city office block, the building appears to diminish. Similarly, a small amount of highlight colour in a room will draw the attention, making the rest of the space appear less important.

too much colour

If you have too much attention-seeking colour the eye will not know where to rest and it will become tired. The result will be a room that feels small, oppressive and over-busy.

you've been framed

The impact of large areas of strong dramatic colours can be lessened by using 'frames' (see 20). If you paint these in a colour to contrast with the wall, they will make the wall seem smaller and will also have an effect on the way the colour of the wall is perceived.

safe and sound

Although pale colours can make a small room seem more spacious add some contrasting colour to avoid an insipid appearance.

panel and position

Panels of colour are a useful way of drawing the eye along a space. For example, if the walls in a long corridor are painted or papered in a pale colour and a door or wall at the end is in a brighter or contrasting colour, the eye will be drawn to the end of the corridor rather than dwelling on its length.

shadow play

Uplights placed on the floor in the corners of a room will have the effect of making the lower part of the room appear dark and the colours there deeper, and the upper part of the wall lighter. The result will be that the room will look taller and wider.

top and bottom

If you opt for the same colour on the floor and ceiling, the top and bottom of the room appear to come closer, making you feel sandwiched or trapped between the two.

lines and alignment

The arrangement of lines affects the way we perceive a space. For example, by running floorboards along the length of a room you exaggerate its length

10 ideas

whereas running the boards across the width of the room will make the room appear wider. The same theory can be applied to stripes with colour – striped wallpaper, painted stripes or striped fabric. In general, the effect is better if length is emphasised rather than width.

the right amount

The colour and pattern of upholstery and the amount of it used in a room will influence the amount of space you feel you have. A large, brightly coloured and patterned two-seater sofa will dominate a small room whereas two armchairs covered in the same fabric will appear less dominant. By giving glimpses of floor and a gap between the chairs, the chairs will look less obvious and space-greedy, whereas the sofa is seen as one solid block.

45
colour for individual rooms

When you are planning a colour scheme for an individual room, you need to consider what the room will be used for and by whom. Rooms that aren't used frequently, for example, a separate dining room, can be decorated in more vivid and unusual colour schemes because they are dipped into from time to time. For rooms that are used much more often and by family and friends alike – for example living rooms, television rooms, kitchens and kitchen-dining rooms – it is best to stick to a neutral or subtly coloured scheme. That way the room will be a place that is comfortable to be in at any time of the day, at various times of the year and for a range of activities such as watching television or holding a conversation or meeting.

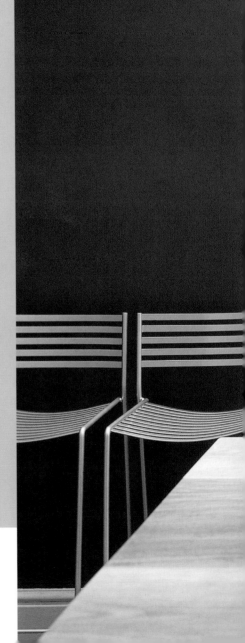

46 colour for living rooms

A living room often hosts a number of activities and provides a background to several different interests, for example, watching television, playing games, conversation, and hobbies such as knitting or reading. It is also a rather public area where you might entertain friends and family, so it needs to be a versatile room with decoration and colours that will lend themselves to all of these uses. A good compromise would be to go for a light, neutral-coloured scheme, perhaps with a single wall of an accent colour and accessories to embellish and create an identity.

Such a busy space will also be subject to wear and tear, especially if it is in a family home, so fabrics and finishes should be sturdy and robust. If upholstery is to be in a pale colour check that the fabric has a stain-repellent finish so that it will be easy to maintain.

colour for kitchen–dining rooms

These days, since separate dining rooms often do not figure in compact, modern homes, many kitchens aren't just used for cooking but are also sociable areas. In the kitchen area the emphasis is on hygiene, for work, while the dining area needs to adapt from family breakfasts to evening suppers for adult friends. Colour can help to link the two zones, with lighting and finishes supplying the change of mood and emphasis.

Kitchens are best decorated with light fresh colours – perhaps choosing a darker shade of the same colour in the dining area – and easy-to-clean surfaces such as ceramic tiles, melamine, Formica, wood and steel. But some of these finishes are too clinical and utilitarian for a dining area so you might prefer to have a change of materials there. For example, you could use ceramic tiles and vinyl paint on the walls of the kitchen and wallpaper in the dining area, and opt for blinds in the kitchen and decorative curtains in the dining area. Remember, too, that a little pattern goes a long way in a work area, so save most of it for the dining section.

You can also emphasise a change in depth of colour between the two areas of the room by your choice of lighting. In the kitchen, you will need more utilitarian lighting – a combination of task lighting, focused on the worktops, and a central or ambient light to give overall illumination – whereas in the dining room you might choose wall lights or recessed halogen spots on a dimmer switch to be supplemented by candlelight during an evening meal. The lighting will add to the effect of the different moods in each room but the link provided by the underlying colour scheme will help to give an impression of unity.

separate dining rooms

If you do have a separate dining room, you have a wider range of decorating options. Because the room will be used most often at night, you could go for rich, dark, dramatic colours . Midnight blue, malachite green and the aptly named Eating Room Red, which is a classic paint colour made by a number of premium-quality brands, are all worth considering. The glamour and luxuriance of glass and mirror and metallics such as silver and gold will be enhanced against colours such as these. Also think about the light in a separate dining room; candlelight will serve to heighten the richness of the colour.

50 colour for children's rooms

Traditionally, nurseries are painted in pastel colours, often following the custom of pink for a girl, blue for a boy and with primrose yellow being a safe bet either way. As children grow, it's common to increase the strength of colour in their rooms too, so that by the time they are toddlers, the walls, bed and toy boxes are often decked out in a punchy palette of primary colours.

But the primaries tend to be stimulating and vibrant (see 37) which isn't necessarily a good thing for a child's bedtime, so look instead at the mid-tones or at the interesting palette of secondary colours such as orange, green and purple. These are still fun but contain a blend of hot and cool elements.

It's a good idea to introduce pattern to a child's room and this can be an inspiration for the colours used elsewhere. Whether you take your palette from a curtain fabric, a wallpaper border, a favourite cartoon character such as Thomas the Tank Engine or a toy such as Barbie who is associated with her own vivid shade of pink, you can use it as a starting point from which to build.

Also take into consideration the location and size of your child's room. Children are often allocated a small room and if the room is at the back of the house because that's quieter, then it may also lack direct sunlight because of adjacent buildings. Take all these factors into consideration when you are making your colour-scheming plans as you may want to steer towards the lighter side of the spectrum to increase the feeling of light and space in the room.

For older children's bedrooms it is usually best to leave the choice of colour to the child or at least discuss it with him or her. For example, teenage children may want a currently fashionable colour, the colours of their favourite sports team or a neutral background onto which they can put posters and their own decoration.

51 colour for the workspace

The colour you choose for your workspace is a personal thing and will depend on how you respond to colour and the size of your room. It may also be influenced by whether you work from home and use the room all the time, or in an office, in which case you will only use the room at home occasionally.

the occasional office

You can decorate an occasional office in a bolder, more colourful scheme than you would use if you were sitting in it all day, every day. Traditionally, studies with book-lined walls were decorated in masculine colours from the darker end of the spectrum, but muted and grey tones are suitable, too. The colours best avoided are pinks and purples; they can be distracting as well as sugary. Also avoid bright yellows as they are generally too invigorating, although mustard and ochre shades can be warming in a dark or cool study.

the home worker

If you work from home but have people coming to visit you on business, you need to create the right impression, so smart, elegant surroundings are important. The room should convey a professional approach but should also be comfortable and relaxing. Green is a fresh, harmonious colour and a pale version of it or a green-tinged apple white as a main colour will create a smart, business-like background. But it's best to avoid fashion greens such as lime – which is over-stimulating – and dull greens like sage because their sludgy overtones are too dreary.

Next pick a highlight colour or colours. Black and white are crisp, clean highlights that are good for a work environment. When it comes to furniture, consider wood. Its earthiness offers some balance to the hi-tech gadgetry of the modern office. Satinwood or ash will harmonise well with your green background, or perhaps choose a wood with a red tint such as rich cherrywood. Red is opposite green on the colour wheel so the two work well together.

Finally, if you work at home try and set a room or separate area aside specifically for work. Keep it organised and uncluttered and do not decorate with overly fussy wallpaper or highly patterned fabrics. Instead, keep the space calm and simple so that your mind can focus on the task in hand.

brighten up the office

If you work in an office, you will have little option but to accept the décor that is there although you may be able to personalise your immediate area. A plant or flower on your desk will add some colour and a coffee mug, filing tray, folder and pen pot in lively colours will make your working environment more stimulating. But all these things should be done in moderation; you don't want your desk to look like a circus of colour in an otherwise neutral oasis of beige.

colour for one-room living

Studio apartments or open-plan flats often have limited space so it's best to make visual, rather than real divisions and to stick to a simple palette of colours. With clever colour scheming, each area of the room can make a different statement.

four tips for one-room schemes

1 • Keep a simple unifying scheme of light and bright tones. The neutrals are ideal for this sort of situation.
2 • Colourful or patterned rugs or mats against a plain floor will focus attention on individual areas.
3 • Mobile walls, screens or bookcases on wheels can be used to create more intimate spaces within the larger one.
4 • Make colour links between the different areas of the space. For example, it could be as simple as grouping sofas and armchairs around a colourful rug and using the rug colour for a wall in the kitchen, or reflecting the colour of pictures on the wall in the sitting area in a vase of flowers on the dining table.

colour for whole-house schemes

Not everyone is in the position of being able to decorate their whole home in one go, but even if you can't, it pays to have an overall plan in your head that you can apply to each room as and when you are ready to decorate.

You might have a favourite colour that you'd like to use in every room, but you should avoid doing this because it can look monotonous. A compromise solution would be to have a core collection of colours based on your favourite (see 14).

This option would also mean that rooms that open off one another would harmonise, which would bring a sense of unity to your home (see 54).

A bolder, more unusual option is to use colour to create different moods in different parts of the house. You might choose an invigorating colour scheme (see 37) in one room to make you feel lively and ready for action and a restful scheme (see 36) in another to help you relax.

Colour can also be used to make rooms more user-friendly at different times of the year and in various seasons; sunny light yellow rooms can be inspiring in the spring and summer whereas rust red or deep pink rooms are warm and comforting in the winter.

colour for hallways, passageways and spaces that link

54

Halls should be inviting so you need to choose colours that will enhance the sense of light and space and make the journey from one end to the other an enjoyable transition.

seven colour-scheming tips

1 • When selecting a colour for a corridor or hallway, take into consideration the adjacent rooms. Off-whites are a good choice because they are neutral and will be compatible with any adjacent colour, whereas, for example, a vibrant orange hall opening onto a purple-pink bedroom and an olive green sitting room will, as you open the doors, make the bedroom seem hotter and the sitting room colour appear sludgy.

2 • Corridors and hallways are often windowless, but you may be able to introduce natural light by putting in a skylight or replacing solid doors with panels of opaque glass so that daylight in the rooms beyond can filter through. The natural light will enhance pale and white-based colours and will lift vivid colours such as orange, yellow and bright red. It will also prevent the deeper colours such as navy and bottle green, from being too black and gloomy.

3 • Light, bright colours will give an impression of airiness and mirrors will add to the effect, amplifying any available natural light as well as doubling the perceived area of colour in a room (see 28).

4 • Orange and red are upbeat colours but in a long, narrow space they may be overwhelming and claustrophobic, whereas mid-tones and pastels will add interest while giving

an impression of colour.

5 • Use a picture rail and/or dado rail to make an interesting feature in a corridor and to break up the wall colour. For example, apply a patterned or textured wallpaper between the skirting board and the dado rail – the area that is most likely to get scuffed or marked – and use a single colour or a compatible striped wallpaper between the dado and picture rail. Finally, use a co-ordinating colour but in a different shade above the picture rail and over the ceiling to finish the scheme.

6 • Hall floors should be easy to maintain and can be gloss-painted, wood-stained in a rich natural mahogany or oak, or colour-stained. You could have a narrow runner in a contrasting or complementary colour along the centre of the floor so there is something soft underfoot in the main area of use – or just fake the appearance of a runner in paint.

7 • Some hallways open out into a bay window or recess where a small sitting area could be created or extra storage installed. If the space is large enough you could make a feature of it by using a contrasting colour and pattern scheme. For example, if the hall walls are plain, you could introduce an area of pattern in complementary colours to the recess or vice versa.

how to get the look – historic colour themes

A large percentage of housing stock is old, made up of some buildings from the nineteenth century, a considerable proportion from the twentieth century and a small proportion of new homes from the twenty-first century. If you have an older home, decorating using the period style associated with the age of your building can be a useful starting point when trying to decide on colour schemes.

Even if you don't want to follow a period style slavishly you can take elements from it to create a hybrid or up-dated version, and colour is a good place to start. Paint manufacturers produce palettes of colours that have been brought together to evoke a certain period or style of décor and these can be used on their own without the period furnishings and accessories. The advantage of taking inspiration from a manufacturer's palette is that you know the colours have been tried and tested and that they will all work well together.

a touch of period style

Following a period style doesn't mean that you have to use it throughout your home; you could just indulge the look in a single room. For example, you might fancy a glamorous Art Deco bathroom with a pink sunken bath reached by

carpeted steps, black-and-pink geometric tiles, champagne-coloured mirrors and angular deco-style lights, or you might yearn for a decadent and lavish boudoir in the eighteenth-century style of Madame de Pompadour.

You could also choose a period of decorative style and a colour palette that isn't necessarily that of your home; for example, there has been a fashionable revival of interest in 1950s and 1960s style which can be used in most settings. Yet another option is to choose classic collections of colours and styles that never go out of date.

The important thing is to find the right balance of period style and modern comfort. A few dedicated people recreate a style right down to authentic bath taps and horsehair-stuffed chairs, but for most of us there is a point where practicality takes priority. That's when the ranges of reproduction or re-edition furniture and accessories and new products inspired by past eras come into their own. They combine the look of a certain period with modern standards such as flame-retardant upholstery, stain-repellent finishes and modern pipe gauging and fitments.

Another option is to choose from the many original items that are still in production today. The fabrics and wallpapers designed by William Morris in the mid-nineteenth century are still being produced, as is furniture designed by Marcel Breuer in the 1930s, chairs of the 1950s such as the Eames armchair model no. 670 and footstool model no. 671, Arne Jacobsen's Series 7 seat and Alvar Aalto's fan-leg stool. All are available in most good modern furniture shops and will sit perfectly alongside a modern sofa or a dining table. In other words, you don't need to be a collector to achieve the look.

the advantages of our modern age

While in centuries gone by colour was the privilege of the wealthy few, with rare pigments such as blue being bought and traded from foreign parts, today we have modern printing techniques and colour production that give us a wide range of paints and finishes and a rainbow selection of fabrics and patterns.

We also have finishes that can emulate techniques that once took hours of skilled labour to produce, for a example, a couple of well-applied coats of gloss paint can look like lacquer, a stencil and template can recreate the look of marquetry and inlay, and even paint finishes such as marbling and verdigris can be bought by the metre on printed wallpapers. It has never been easier to create your own historic theme.

the nineteenth century

This period covers the late eighteenth-century styles through to the first decade of the twentieth century, and spans the delicate, refined palette of the neo-classical style to the full-blown richness and embellishment of high Victoriana.

The neo-classical period runs from the mid-eighteenth to the mid-nineteenth century and one of its greatest exponents was Robert Adam. The style he perfected was inspired by classical Greek and Roman design and spread across Europe, Scandinavia and America.

From the mid-1800s a palette of richer, darker colours became fashionable and was used in densely patterned wallpapers, tiles, upholstery material, carpets and curtain fabrics. Trimming such as tassels, fringes and braids were used to further embellish pelmets, cloths and rich mahogany furniture.

Gothic Revival and Federal style were also part of this period. The Gothic Revival saw the re-emergence of pointed arches and window frames, tapestry and decorative encaustic tiles inspired by the Middle Ages. This was a look that Augustus Pugin championed and used in his work on the interior of the Palace of Westminster in London. The Federal style, which featured in American interiors of this period, combined elements of Adam-style neo-classicism with certain borrowings from the French Empire style.

key colours, materials and features

- in the neo-classical period – white-based colours, pale and medium greens, lilac and pink, pale orange, grey and blue; white plaster; ornate friezes of white and gilded plasterwork columns, panels of bas-relief
- in Gothic Revival and Federal – bottle green, taupe, saffron yellow and French navy blue with off-white or ivory panels, cornices and plaster details
- in the latter part of the nineteenth century – bottle green, crimson red, indigo blue and mustard yellow; dark-coloured woods such as teak and mahogany; lots of pattern, trimmings and decoration; rich, heavy fabrics

gustavian 57

This Swedish style started in the late eighteenth century and includes elements of neo-classicism in its make-up. However, the look in its purest form is so simple and clean that it has a timelessness which is adaptable to most settings. This has meant that its popularity remains undiminished today.

For an intimate view of a domestic interior that incorporates elements of Gustavian style look at the charming watercolour paintings of 'Ett Hem' (a home), the family house in Sundban of the late-nineteenth-century artist Carl Larsson.

Although the backdrop to the Gustavian look is plain, pattern was introduced in over-painting on walls, floors and furniture and through fabrics. To lift what could become a bland background, sections of wall were often painted to appear as panelling and small motifs of floral swags and bows were painted on chairbacks or as a frieze along a wall. Fabrics were usually simple gingham checks, ticking stripes and toile de Jouy, all with white backgrounds.

Displays of daintily decorated china, often in plate racks and on dressers were a favoured accessory. Tiles, again with white or off-white backgrounds, were used in many areas of the home and often as a cladding or façade for stoves and fireplaces, which were often positioned across the corner of a room.

key colours, materials and features
• chalky and pale colours, predominantly white or off-white; patterned over-painting in warm, pink-hued hyacinth blue, grey, green, lilac and red
• walls often wood-panelled
• floors invariably planked and largely left bare
• rag rugs and runners in white, blue, red, lilac and pink on plain or painted wooden floors
• furniture predominantly wood, painted or limewashed in similar pale shades to the walls

shaker 58

The Shakers, or United Society of Believers in the First and Second appearance of Christ, were nineteenth-century America's largest communal utopian society. Although only half a dozen or so Shakers remain today, the Shaker legacy and simple style of homeliness lives on.

What inspired the décor of the communal homes in which the Shakers lived was practicality. One of their favoured hymns was 'The Gift to Be Simple' and a saying of their founder Mother Ann Lee was 'Put your hands to work and your heart to God'.

But practical didn't mean dull. The Shakers loved colour and wove colourful webbing tapes from home-dyed yarns of yellow, red, blue, green and brown. These were used to fill the seat frames of their cherrywood chairs, while on larger looms they made decorative blankets and coverlets in checks and geometric patterns in colours similar to those of the webbing tapes.

The simplicity and quality of the things the Shakers made have withstood the test of time. Their tall, elegant and practical ladder-back chairs, which can be hung on peg rails around the room so that the floor can be quickly and efficiently swept, are still found in the hallways and lobbies of modern homes. Copies are available from many furniture manufacturers. In addition, their wooden storage boxes with dovetail joints and their baskets that were used to store everything from grain and flour to sewing threads are still in production.

The Shaker style has also been adapted to encompass modern settings; contemporary microwave ovens and ceramic hobs are fitted into Shaker-style kitchens which use the simple panelling favoured by the religious community as well as their strong palette of colours mixed with natural polished woods.

key colours, materials and features
- ox-blood red, sage green and grey-blue
- simplicity and practicality
- peg rails
- oval wooden boxes
- tall ladder-back chairs with acorn finials

oriental influences and chinoiserie

Chinoiserie is the name given to the western interpretation of Chinese and Japanese furnishings, artefacts and ornamentation. Its influence started in the eighteenth century when porcelain, silk and lacquer began to be more extensively imported from China and Japan. It captured the European imagination, especially that of the English Prince Regent, who incorporated chinoiserie in his famous pavilion at Brighton.

In the early nineteenth century, British potters started to produce large quantities of Chinese-influenced factory-made ceramics, the most popular of which was the Willow Pattern. Furniture was 'Japanned' to imitate lacquer, and mother-of-pearl inlay and imitation pearlised materials were fashionable.

Oriental style – especially ebonising, lacquerware and embroidered silks – became popular again in the 1920s as a complement to Art Deco. Taste once again turned eastward at the end of the twentieth century with the interest in Zen and Feng Shui. Zen, in particular, with its paring down of belongings and objects, influenced minimalism in the home.

key colours, materials and features
- pearly white, celadon green, almond blossom pink, ivory and black
- bamboo motifs, especially trompe l'oeil interpretations
- willow pattern china
- lacquerware
- screens and carvings of temple dogs and lions
- embroidered silks

art nouveau

Art Nouveau was a modernist movement that reacted against the dogma, history and tradition of the nineteenth century. It started at the end of the old century, around 1880, and rushed into the new, fading out around the start of the First World War in 1914.

The aim of the Art Nouveau movement was to produce designs of high quality by machine. The forms were characterised by asymmetry and stylised flower and leaf motifs which often featured in great swathes of curling wrought iron, made into balconies, window grilles and balustrades.

There were leading exponents of this new look Europe-wide; they included the Belgian architect and designer Victor Horta, Scottish architect and designer Charles Rennie Macintosh, the Spanish architect Antonio Gaudí, Austrian artist Gustav Klimt and French glass-makers René Lalique and Emile Galle.

key colours, materials and features
- peacock blues, purple, jade and mint greens
- bronze, brass, lead and pewter.
- organic shapes
- sinuous curves as well as dramatic straight, angular lines

art deco 61

Art Deco – the name came from a Paris exhibition of decorative arts in 1925 – sprang from the Jazz Age. Its feel was fresh, new and dynamic. The influences on it were Cubism and Fauvism, as well as the work of individual painters such as Matisse. The German Bauhaus Institute, founded in 1919 by Walter Gropius, also provided inspiration in the style of functional architecture it developed and the use of experimental building materials it pioneered.

The materials popularised by Bauhaus designers were increasingly the new man-made materials, such as plastics, used alongside utilitarian surfaces such as glass and metal.

In applied decoration black lacquer and gloss surfaces were popular. The amazing discovery of Tutankhamen's tomb in 1922 started a cult of Egyptian-inspired decoration and this fed into the Art Deco style, too.

key colours, materials and features
• black and white, pink, champagne, apricot and mint green
• chrome, glass and mirror.
• geometric and abstract shapes
• boxy furniture
• bevelled-edge mirrors

modern 62

The Modern movement, which started between the First and Second World Wars, was a continuation of the teachings of the Bauhaus movement. The style rejected superfluity; it was a minimalist, angular look that favoured flat-roofed buildings made

of concrete, glass and metal, especially steel. The palette was white and neutral with polished hardwood, rubber or cork-covered floors, steel-frame casement windows and glass bricks used as partitions and internal walls.

In these pared-down settings furniture became a decorative feature and streamlined chrome and aluminium furniture with black leather upholstery, by designers such as Le Corbusier and Eileen Gray, came into vogue. Marcel Breuer's Wassily chair and Mies van der Rohe's Barcelona chair, both from this period, are still in demand today. The other designer from this era whose work is still sought after is Alvar Aalto. This Finnish designer pioneered work with laminates and plywood, using veneers and bonding to create durable yet lightweight furniture with more organic forms than the strict lines of other designers at the time.

key colours, materials and features
- monotone – black and white, concrete grey
- chrome and aluminium
- wood in pale, ashen shades
- simple angular forms
- sculpturally inspired furniture.

fifties and sixties 63

Although the term 'New Look' was originally coined for Christian Dior's fashion collection of 1947, it went on to encompass the interior design, architecture and furnishings of the post-war period.

After years of austerity, there was a burst of energy and enthusiasm for a new look with lots of colour. Unusual and quirky designs were popular and many furnishing-fabric and wallpaper designs were inspired by science. Hans Wegner designed three-legged chairs, Ray Eames and Lucienne Day created fabric prints that looked as though they were hand-drawn and painted onto the fabric, and artists such as Henry Moore and Barbara Hepworth created textile designs for Heal's and other leading British furniture stores.

During this period the applied arts reached a new high. Ceramics and glassware, even cutlery, became artworks, with Picasso creating plates and vases that featured his love of colour as well as figurative designs.

There were hothouses of design in Sweden, Denmark, Finland, Italy and the USA that had a wide-ranging influence and manufacturers such as Herman Miller, Ercol and Knoll made the products widely available and affordable.

The post-war enthusiasm for colour carried through to the next decade when it really blossomed. The 1960s were a time of anti-design, embracing eclecticism and individualism. It is said that during this decade there wasn't really a discernable style; style was more an attitude.

One influence of the 1960s was Flower Power or the hippie movement which embraced a culture of free love and peace. This was translated into interiors filled with beanbags, printed Indian textiles and swirling, floral and candystripe patterns in a rainbow assortment of colours and shades.

Another influence was Pop Art, originating in England and America in the late 1950s and early 1960s. Artists such as David Hockney, Peter Blake, Andy Warhol and Ray Lichtenstein developed a comic-strip style of illustration and used commercial products such as soup cans and Coca-Cola bottles as subjects. Pop-era materials such as PVC and plastic were popular in interiors along with vivid cartoon colours.

key colours, materials and features
• in the 1950s, dynamic, multiple colour; brilliant yellow and red; muted eggshell blues and olive green; black and white for detailing and graphic lines
• in the 1960s, psychedelic colours and fluorescents; orange, shocking pink, bush-baby brown, purple and lilac
• asymmetry; abstract and organic forms; dense patterns and motifs incorporating several colours and shades

how to get the look – travel themes

Travel has inspired decorating schemes for generations of home-owners, whether as a result of people actually travelling to a foreign country and spending time there or through imported products. This was true of the neo-classic look (see 56) and Chinoiserie (see 59), both of which were influenced by places on trade routes, and whose products were brought back by ship.

The Grand Tour, a trip of continental Europe considered part of the education of upper-class young men in the late eighteenth century, saw the arrival of holiday mementoes – the souvenir. These were usually copies of sculptures, paintings of views, rugs, carpets and lengths of locally woven cloths, all prized possessions that were incorporated into the homes of the travellers.

These days travel is more widely enjoyed and takes us more frequently to foreign places. Sometimes we wish to emulate the look of a place we have visited, sometimes we simply want to conjure up an atmosphere or an association by means of certain colours or artefacts.

With travel-inspired decorative themes it is very important to check the quality of light in your room; the wonderful warm terracotta walls of a Tuscan farmhouse or the vibrant pinks and yellows found in the walls and printed cottons of the Caribbean look great in the full sunshine of a southern summer, but may look drab or acidic in the cool, blue wintry light of a northern winter.

Also think about how far you want to take the travel-inspired theme; you should make it work for you and your home rather than becoming a slave to authenticity and correctness. You can adapt and adopt certain elements that will create an essence of the style rather than produce an exact replica.

65

caribbean / tutti frutti

One of the most vibrant colour palettes is the one inspired by the Caribbean, more specifically the islands of Jamaica, Antigua, St Lucia, Barbados, and Trinidad and Tobago. As well as native colour and influences, there are colonial references throughout the islands – that of the French in Martinique, the Spanish and British in Jamaica and the Portuguese in Barbados. Hints of these various imported cultures remain, along with the lace-like cut-out decoration on the barge-board fronts of the pastel-painted wooden houses with their long verandas.

The Caribbean colour palette is picked from the lush vegetation, sun-filled tropical skies, turquoise waters of the ocean and the silvery sand beaches. Think also of the brightly printed fabrics worn by the local people and the cornucopia of fruits that grow there.

The islands are home to colourful fishing villages with their wooden houses often raised up on platforms and with brightly painted boats moored alongside. The colours of these homes are rich, relating to the vivid blue of the sky and sea, and the rich reds and pinks of bougainvillaea, while from the seashore comes the softer option of the pinks, reds and pearly greys of seashells and coral, and the off-whites found in the glistening silver sand.

key colours, materials and features
• indigenous fruit colours – the mellow yellow of bananas, the citrus zest of lemons, oranges and grapefruits, the pinkish-orange of papaya
• the lush greens of vegetation
• the rich azure blue of the sky and sea
• the off-white tones of the sandy beaches
• printed batik and tie-dye fabrics
• rough wooden furniture painted in rich hues

tuscan66

Tuscany, the region of central west Italy inhabited since pre-Roman time, is rich in history and culture. Many of the colours associated with this area are named after the places whose soil and ores were the sources of colour. For example, raw sienna is a reddish pigment that comes from the iron- and manganese-rich earth around the town of Siena. When roasted in a furnace, the pigment becomes richer, darker and more brilliant and is then known as burnt sienna. The clay, sand and minerals of the region also provide umber, a greenish-brown colour, yellow ochre, a muddy mustard yellow, and the warm orange-hued terracotta.

Walls and surfaces in this part of Italy are painted with these pigment finishes or with the paint equivalent, and tend to be matt with graduated, uneven washes of colour that give a time-worn, sun-baked appearance. Floor and roof tiles are made from the local red clay which is baked and sometimes glazed, or finished with a wax or oil seal that heightens the richness of its natural red colouring.

Fabrics are often dyed and printed in greens, blues and lavenders – inspired by the vines, olives and fields of lavender that grow in the region. These cooler colours soften the warmth of the earthy reds and yellows and are often found in simple striped and geometric patterns. Fabrics such as these can be seen in the flags and banners used in The Palio – the medieval horse races run around the centre of Siena twice each summer.

key colours, materials and features
- terracotta and rich red earthy tones, muted yellow, grape and olive greens, strong earthy brown
- terracotta floor and roof tiles
- simple printed fabrics in stripes or panels of colour

provença67l

Many of the colours and influences of the Tuscan palette are shared by the palette inspired by Provence in south-east France. The Mediterranean climate and lifestyle influence both regions, as do the colours of the earth and of local produce, such as wine and fruit.

But Provençal colours tend to be cleaner and stronger, with lavender, often used on doors and shutters, as the key shade, rather than terracotta. Textiles are an important part of this look, and they are generally more colourful and patterned than their Italian neighbours. Curtains, cloths and bedcovers have distinctive Provençal prints, often incorporating motifs depicting branches of black olives with sprigs of leaves and a teardrop-shaped Paisley pattern.

Indigo blue – the same dye that's used to colour denim, or serge de Nîmes, named after the Provençal town – is used not only to dye fabrics but also for colour washes and wall colours. The slightly sharper blue, often referred to as gitane blue from the packaging of the French cigarettes of that name, is also popular and is seen regularly in the ubiquitous overalls of the French ouvrier or workman.

While Tuscan style has its typical mustard-yellow ochre, the Provençal yellow is brighter and crisper; it is more the colour of the glorious sunflowers that fill countless fields in the area. Ceramics often have a yellow or rich cream glaze, and a bright, almost apple green is commonly found over bases of terracotta.

key colours, materials and features
• lavender, indigo blue, sunflower yellow, olive green
• paisley and floral print fabrics
• green and cream glazed earthenware

moroccan

The colours of this North African country are rich and vibrant, inspired by the various blues of the Atlantic Ocean bordering it to the north and the sandy tones of the vast Sahara desert to the south.

Common architectural features include archways and wooden fretwork screens and shutters. These allow cool breezes to flow through and provide some shelter from the heat of the mid-day sun, which creates patterns and shadows as it passes through the lattice openings. Marble is also commonly used on floors as well as window frames and doorways and is prized not just for its hardwearing efficiency but also for its coolness.

Traditional furniture focuses on the daybed and cushions, which easily translate into the modern sofa and ottoman or footstool. Hand-woven carpets and rugs are an important feature of Moroccan homes and often incorporate geometric shapes and stripes in their patterns. They are used in numerous ways, as wall hangings, table covers, on floors, and for upholstery and cushions.

Copper and brass, often decoratively pierced, are frequently used for trays, teapots, lamps and incense burners.

key colours, materials and features
• cobalt, ultramarine, cerulean ocean blue, sandy desert shades from pinkish red to gold, vivid orange, also carmine or madder red and green, but green used sparingly and with care as it is a holy colour in Islam
• ceramics, especially tiles
• dense patterns
• stars, ziggurats and other geometric shapes

japanese

The colours of this palette are influenced by the materials used in the construction of the traditional Japanese home – wood and paper – and by the doctrine of Zen, the meditative Buddhist sect which teaches that 'man's possessions are his burdens' and that there is 'profundity in simplicity'. The interiors that endorse this doctrine are calm, minimalist spaces.

The palette for this look is subtle and concentrates on cleanliness and simplicity. Tatami mats cover most floors and their pristine appearance is maintained by people removing their shoes at the door and walking on the mats in socked feet.

Against this simple background, touches of colour are added by Zen-inspired accessories – perhaps a single prized vase, a glass bowl of water filled with a smooth grey stone or a single branch of almond blossom in a bamboo holder. The philosophy behind such simplicity is that, because only a single item is on display at any one time, it allows that item to be the focus of attention. So, instead of looking at a mixed bunch of flowers in a highly patterned bowl, we can observe and appreciate the detail and intricacy of a single bloom.

Fabrics follow a natural theme, with silk and fine cotton popular, often in white or single colours such as indigo. The combination of indigo and white is also used to create the distinctive ikat designs that are popular in Japan.

key colours, materials and features

- rich ox-blood red, pale celadon green, black, white
- ceramics
- red or black lacquerware
- dark wood
- paper screens
- tatami matting
- simplicity and lack of clutter
- versatile use of space

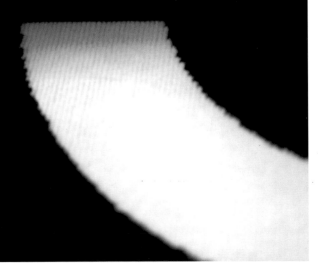

70 log-cabin style

The cabins that inspired this look can be found in various interpretations in North America, Russia, Sweden, Lapland, Finland, Italy and France. They were built by early settlers, woodsmen and trappers using the materials that were most readily available – invariably wood – but to transpose the look to a modern home you must edit and adapt rather than mimic slavishly.

You can easily bring wood into your scheme with wooden furniture and tongue-and-groove planking. This is an ideal floor covering but could also be used as a feature on a single wall. Don't over-do the wood but complement it with a simple palette of paint colours such as off-white or natural tones. Exposed brick and stone, especially around fireplaces, also work well in this context.

For soft furnishings the focus should be on natural materials and homespun or rustic fabrics. Simple prints and patterns would have been used sparingly and were often embroidered.

Originally, nothing went to waste. Horns and hooves became candle holders and knife handles, and the hides of animals were used as bedcovers, throws and even draught-excluders, but these days woollen blankets and rugs make acceptable alternatives. Use handwoven designs with geometric motifs on floors, as wall hangings or even as upholstery. Blankets don't need to be restricted to beds either; they can be hung as curtains from wooden curtain poles by means of chunky leather ties or large brass rings.

Local crafts and skills were invariably employed in the furnishing of the original homes and there are quirky details and finishes that are special to each region. The decoration of the dwelling would also reflect the personality of the owner; a sea-dog whose cabin was by the coast might have hung fishing nets and pieces of driftwood on the walls, whereas a hill walker or mountain man might have feathers and pine cones on his mantelpiece. These are ideas that you could emulate to bring your own interests and personality into the mix.

key colours, materials and features

• wood and earth tones, highlight colours of red and green
• creamy cottons
• practical, durable, unfussy but comfortable
• traders blankets, fur – fake is more acceptable these days
• painted tinware
• old tools, old copper and enamel kitchenware

the ethnic mix

Due to the increasing globalisation of the world you can buy ethnic goods over the internet, from your corner shop or from a department store in town, so your home can be decorated to look as though you have travelled the world while in reality you haven't stepped much beyond your front door.

This melting-pot style is truly of our time and it also highlights the versatility of modern manufacture. You can go into a shop and buy a bowl that looks as though it was hand-thrown by a village potter in the south of France but in fact came off a production line in Turkey. Equally, you can find a kelim or rug that appears to have travelled the trade route from Samarkand but was really run up in a factory in Romania. Things are not necessarily as they seem.

As long as you can find a common theme or colour to bring this mix together and to give it some sort of order, the results in your home should be cohesive. For example, the red-and-black rugs of Morocco have an affinity with the russet lacquerware of Japan and will also blend with a mottled cream-and-grey-feathered African head-dress. Set them off against a matt, cadmium-red wall, add some black leather and dark wood furniture, and together they will create an interior with plenty of impact and interest.

Blue-and-white colour schemes are another good choice for rooms decorated with a mix of different ethnic items. The colour indigo is one that has travelled far around the world and ikat-dyed fabrics using indigo are found in Africa and Asia as well as in France and India. Combine these fabrics with some of the many blue-and-white ceramics – contemporary or traditional – that are made all over the world and you have the basis for a colour scheme that will very successfully unify an ethnic collection.

key colours, materials and features

- a diverse palette
- groups and arrangements of objects that form 'families' linked by colour or a common shape or aspect

how to get the look – contemporary themes

Contemporary style evolves around us and increasingly our homes are about us as individuals and the way we live rather than having a single definitive look. For the majority of people, home is a mix of styles and furniture – a few inherited pieces, some chain-store buys and several things of which we are really proud. The trick is to find a setting in which all these things sit comfortably and the choice often comes down to whether you decide to do up rooms in different colours and themes or whether you have the same backdrop throughout your home but furnish with a disparate collection of possessions.

The trends that have arisen recently embrace a number of influences from the stark whiteness of minimalism to lively colourful ethnic and, most commonly, eclectic. Eclectic is defined by the dictionary as 'borrowing from different sources, not exclusive in one taste', which describes the accumulative bits and pieces that many home-owners gather around them.

The standard three-piece suite with matching armchairs seems to have been overtaken by collections of individual seats and stools, sometimes a mix of recent classics from designers such as Ron Arad or Matthew Hilton together with a couple of bucket chairs from Ikea and a chaise longue found in a local second-hand shop and recovered.

The separate dining room with formal table and matching chairs has more or less been lost and replaced by the kitchen–dining or living–dining space and as a consequence of this transition, dining furniture and table settings have become lighter and less formal.

So instead of slavishly following one specific style, the contemporary approach is to put together a selection of things that suit you, choose colours that please you and complement your belongings, and seek inspiration from a wide variety of sources.

classic white

The white-box room is the epitome of minimalism and is almost an icon of late twentieth- and early twenty-first-century design. The work of architects such as John Pawson and Claudio Silvestrin led the way in minimalism and resulted in the acceptance and then imitation of this pure, ascetic living space.

The secret to the minimalist room is to adopt the Zen approach to clutter – which is to do away with it. And, to accommodate the belongings that you do retain in ample and cleverly concealed storage. The edict is 'less is more' so that the less furniture and fewer accessories you have, the more space there is in which to walk and move around. This unhindered space is perceived as an antidote to the fuss and bustle of metropolitan life.

The look is not about quantity but about quality. Since the eye is not distracted by many disparate elements in the room, it lingers on what is there and as a result, every detail and finish must be perfect and any object that is displayed should be the best or most admirable of its type. So, for example, a single red tulip in a glass can become the primary decoration.

Nor does the white-box room have to be limited to contemporary furniture and accessories. It can also provide a dramatic background against which to set prize pieces of antique furniture. The richness of mellow, aged wood, intricate carvings and details are all the more noticeable because there is nothing to distract from them,

especially if the upholstery in the room is also plain white, in a fabric such as linen or calico.

But the discipline required to live in the ultimate white space is too much for most people. It is a demanding regime to live with and furniture and upholstery must be maintained to a high standard, so although people often admire the spirit of minimalism, they usually opt for a less strict arrangement. They take elements from minimalism such as its clean, angular lines and white background, but they adapt it to suit their own requirements. The result is often that firstly, the pure white is softened to off-white and then, increasingly, a single wall or panel of colour is introduced into the space.

key colours, materials and features

- white
- clean open spaces
- few well chosen pieces of furniture
- hidden storage

metallica

Contemporary schemes that include metallic finishes vary widely. The current love of professional kitchens and their utilitarian, industrial-style equipment has seen the rise of steel finishes in the domestic kitchen. In domestic settings, their clinical appearance is often softened with the addition of colour and wood. Zesty orange and green can provide a bright counterbalance, but colours with a warming hint of red are often more comfortable to live with.

Metallic finishes are popular in other parts of the modern home, too. Copper, silver and gold-leaf finishes can also be found (see 33). Wallpapers printed to look as though the surface has been covered with hundreds of individual sheets of metal leaf are very effective. These make extremely dramatic panels in hallways and corridors, especially if they are lit by downlights to enhance their metallic sheen.

Metal-thread curtains and fabrics can also be used to add lustre to a room and can subtly lift the sameness of a single-colour scheme or a tone-on-tone scheme. Fine silver- or pewter-coloured fabric can be used to great effect as a room divider or instead of a muslin or voile curtain at a window. The greyish metallic look of the fabric gives it an opaque quality which obscures or distances a view, but will still allow a certain amount of light, whether natural or electric, to pass through.

key colours, materials and features
• cool silvery tones, warm gold, copper and brass
• shiny and matt surfaces used in moderation as a highlight or practical feature

dark – the new glamour

As a reaction against the sugary pink and pastel colours that have, until recently, had connotations of girlie glamour, the new interpretation of glamour is more mature and has embraced the deeper, richer, blacker end of the spectrum.

Taking inspiration from the 1930s Art Deco period (see 61), the look uses a lot of gloss and lacquer, but rather than black being the primary shade, the favoured tones are deep red, purple and brown.

Mirror mosaics and furniture with facings and surfaces covered with panels of mirror are a must for the glamorous boudoir, as is Perspex, which looks like glass but is more user-friendly and adds an ethereal, fairytale look to chairs and tables. Chandeliers are back in a big way, too, but not just the classic crystal chandeliers. Instead there are tumbling mixed-coloured cascades or chandeliers in stylised forms such as plump bunches of glass grapes.

Fabrics for the new glamour look are glossy silks and satins as well as embossed and over-printed velvets, while additional quilting and embroidery in silk or metal threads gives even the most mundane fabrics an expensive appearance. Fake furs add a decadent touch as do tassels, fringing and beaded and sequinned braids.

If you prefer your glamour on a lighter note opt for cream or white as your main shade. Metallic and glass finishes will still sparkle but the overall look will be less of an imposition in a more public or shared space.

key colours, materials and features
• burgundy red with splashes of golden yellow and apple green; rich purples with raspberry; lilac and chocolate brown with copper and luscious cream and toffee colours
• shine – from silk to mirror and glass (it's difficult to over-dress!)

pastels

Pastels have to be treated with care or they can look insipid; pink, in particular, should be tried out to ensure that you don't get a sickly sugary shade. Modern pastels are generally used in tone-on-tone schemes so that they are part of a range of shades rather than the sole colour. By using the pastel in conjunction with lighter and darker tones you get an interesting layered effect which gives depth to the scheme.

Pastels look fresh and inviting and can work well in stripes. For example, a mint green-and-pink stripe with intermittent bands of white has a summery appearance.

Pastel blues and yellows, the colours favoured by the artist Monet at his home in Giverny, are also cheerful and sunny. Pastel blue and green used together are suggestive of water and make a sparkling combination for a bathroom or cloakroom.

A contemporary way of creating a pastel finish on walls or wooden furniture is to use a watercolour effect – a wash of a colour which, when brushed over a white or off-white base, gives a pleasant and gentle essence of the undiluted colour.

Pastel-coloured fabrics are effective as curtains or blinds, because they don't cut down the light as much as richer-coloured materials. They look especially attractive in voiles because they add just a hint of colour to the light passing through them, which can give a sunny or rosy hue to a room.

Because of their pale nature, pastels are not ideal shades for upholstery; they will easily become marked or stained, unless finished with a stain-repellent finish. But an occasional or decorative chair which is not subjected to heavy daily use, can look attractive upholstered in a pastel-coloured fabric.

key colours, materials and features
- white-based or watery shades – pink, powder blue, pale green, lilac, primrose
- can be teamed with a deeper shade of the base colour for a tone-on-tone effect, for example powder blue with navy blue.

fresh

Most modern home-owners seek space and light and using a scheme of fresh colours helps to bring these elements into the home. The fresh palette is a balance of off-whites or neutrals with other colours. These colours can be influenced by fashion, so are subject to frequent changes and updates which can be capitalised on to refresh the appearance of the room from time to time. The neutral background provides the perfect backdrop for the changes because it accommodates any colour set against it.

One typical and popular combination of colour in the fresh palette is white with dark brown and orange; this is a dramatic combination but works well in homes of most periods. The white gives a light, neutral base for the walls, the dark brown, used on floors and woodwork, gives balance and weight, and the orange – from the same colour family as the brown – is the highlight shade. If the orange is used for a range of accessories – glassware, cushions, throws, and so on – it is easy to change the room's appearance when it begins to look tired and worn or when fashions change.

In a room such as a kitchen or bathroom where sinks, ovens and baths are more or less permanent fixtures, a fresh theme can be based around white or off-white walls and the furniture and accessories can do the decorating, for example, stools with brightly coloured seats at the breakfast bar and colourful storage jars on the worktop. You could also add an unusual or retro-styled refrigerator in pink or red which is sure to be a point of interest.

key colours, materials and features

• white or off-white, black, chocolate brown; highlights of red, lime green, brilliant blue, orange
• single wall of a vibrant colour
• accessories, especially glass and china, are important

78 the colour's in the detail

Although the main impact of colour, when you walk into a room, comes from the walls and the larger pieces of furniture, the colours chosen for the details are an important contributory factor. The overall appearance of the room is the sum of all the individual elements, from the skirting boards and window frames to the radiators and the curtain trims and accessories.

top tip

When planning your scheme, start with the larger areas but don't run out of steam when it comes to the minutiae. Even the door handles and window catches, lampshades and picture frames are important ingredients. Think of it as making a cake; every gram of flour, sugar and butter is vital to produce a successful result.

79 walls

Choosing a wall colour is probably the most important decision you'll have to make in your colour scheming because the walls create the first and biggest impact as you enter a room. The wall colour will also influence the choice of finish for the ceiling and floor as well as for the window treatments and upholstery.

And don't forget that the colour on your walls doesn't have to come only from paint. Wallpapers in every conceivable colour – including metallics, fabrics and natural fibres – and in every conceivable pattern are widely available and can be used to give either a neutral background or a bolder effect, possibly on just one wall or in an alcove.

In kitchens and bathrooms, much of the colour will come from tiling or splashbacks, plus the wall cabinets. Together, these surfaces offer an endless range of possibilities – ceramic tiles in all the colours of the rainbow and every design imaginable, and cabinets in woods of various hues, in frosted glass, and in metal and laminates.

and now for something different

An unusual alternative to a single colour on all the walls is to opt for two shades from the same base. These can be used to create interesting effects, for example, three walls could be painted in the lighter shade but the wall opposite the window, or a wall containing the chimneybreast and fireplace, could be painted in the darker shade. In this way the attention is focused on the dark wall, which gives the room an interesting perspective.

ceilings

The colour you select for the ceiling in your room will be influenced by its height, the size of the room and the available light. A small room with a tall ceiling might look more in proportion if the ceiling is painted in a darker or warmer shade, which will make it appear closer. If the room is large with a low ceiling, then white or a light, cool colour will help to make it appear farther away.

four choices for ceilings

1 • Colour that contrasts with the walls. Opt for a colour that is darker than the walls, maybe even a rich gloss or lacquer finish, which gives a dramatic effect. These shiny surfaces act like a mirror and reflect the light, especially electric light, so creating the impression that the ceiling is infinitesimal, receding into the distance.

2 • Colour that matches the walls. If you choose this option, avoid the space becoming box-like by having the floor in a darker, more grounding, colour. If possible, create a break – perhaps a piece of contrast-painted plaster or fibreboard moulding – between the ceiling and walls and paint the skirting board in a contrast colour, too.

3 • Colour that is slightly lighter or darker than the walls. For example, in a room with plasterwork details, such as cornicing and a central ceiling rose, it can be very effective to have a tonal scheme, with the ceiling slightly darker than the walls and the plasterwork picked out in white or off-white.

4 • Wallpaper or pattern. If you have a tall room and an otherwise simple scheme it can be dramatic to use a mottled paint-effect or wallpaper with a simple pattern on the ceiling, but it should be balanced by a single-coloured floor-covering or rug.

floors

A floor is more open to colour variations than a ceiling because there are more materials to choose from. Your choice will depend on your preferences, but also on practicality. In a hallway, for example, the priority will be to find a material and colour that withstand wear and tear. In a kitchen, you will be looking for a floor that is easy to clean and maintain. Here a light colour is often a better choice because you can readily identify where spills and drips have occurred. A pale floor will also reflect light which will make the kitchen brighter.

As a general rule, a floor should be in a slightly darker colour to the rest of the room. This is not only for practical reasons but also because it gives a sense of a 'base' or 'bottom' to the room. In 'designer-speak', it 'grounds a colour scheme'.

wood

This comes in a wide range of colours from the white and yellow of ash and pine to the rich warmth of cherrywood and mahogany. Remember that if you wax or varnish wood the colour will intensify and in some cases, darken.

But you don't have to stop at natural colours. Wood can be painted in any colour you choose or colourwashed for a lighter effect or, if you are artistic, you can add a painted design.

stone

Stone flooring comes in many colour ranges. There is marble – in a variety of colours from green to rich russet reds, greys, blacks and white; slate – mostly grey and grey-green of varying hues; and limestone and sandstone with their off-white greyness and soft yellowness.

ceramic tile

The sky's the limit here with ceramic tiles in a rainbow assortment of colours, in matt, gloss and mid-sheen finishes. They can be plain or patterned, machine- or hand-made and in sizes from mosaic to paving slab which can be mixed and matched to form patterns and designs.

carpet and rugs

Another flooring where anything goes. Carpets and rugs can be found plain or patterned, smooth or textured and in styles and colours to suit any type of scheme – and don't forget animal-hide and flokati, too.

natural fibres

These embrace fibres such as sisal, coir, jute, seagrass, paper and bamboo. Their overall effect is usually one of neutral colour, but you can also find them dyed in colours ranging from red and green to blue and tan and sometimes edged with contrast binding of cloth or leather.

linoleum

One of the most environmentally friendly flooring materials you can buy, linoleum has made a comeback and it no longer conjures up images of two-tone brown parquet effect drabness. Today you can buy linoleum in every colour under the sun and with surface textures too, if you like.

vinyl

Vinyl tiles come in a vast range of colours and finishes, from matt black and white through 'mock' marbles and faux woods to fantasy designs with hologram effects. Vinyl tiles can be laid in a solid colour, for a checquerboard effect or cut and pieced together to form intricate patterns similar to those of Roman mosaic artists.

cork

In its natural state, cork has a pleasant golden-brown colour, but it may be

stained to give darker shades of brown as well as a range of more unusual colours such as red, green and blue. Its mottled appearance will give it an uneven final colour. Cork should be well sealed as it is absorbent and will soak up any water.

concrete

Concrete in its original state is a greyish, rather bland colour with a matt finish but it can be made more colourful with dyes and pigments in colours ranging from terracotta hues to charcoal grey. These are added to the dry concrete mix. You should bear in mind that the concrete's intrinsic greyness will affect the final colour. Marble dust may also be blended in to give a whiter appearance and a shinier finish.

82
pipes and radiators

Pipes and radiators are increasingly disappearing from sight by being located behind skirting boards and under the floor, but for those of you who still have to contend with them, there are a number of options.

four ways to deal with pipework and radiators

1 • Paint them to match the wall so that they appear to vanish. You can buy specialist radiator paint or use a

matching gloss, eggshell, satin sheen or flat oil finish.

2 • Paint them to match the woodwork, especially if they are located close to doors or under windows. This will make them part of the general framing features of the room.

3 • Turn them into a feature. Many modern radiators are designed to be decorative and don't need any special treatment and in industrial-style spaces, home-owners often like to leave the pipework exposed to endorse the utilitarian roots of the location. In these situations, shining, solid copper pipe, treated with a non-tarnish varnish or protective coating, looks attractive. Reclaimed or reproduction radiators are another popular alternative. These can be sprayed in a copper- or bronze-effect paint or enamel to enhance their appearance and highlight their ornate features.

4 • Conceal them behind a purpose-built cover. These have a metal mesh or pierced wooden panel at the front to allow the warmth to permeate the room. The wood can be painted to blend with or complement the room's wall colour.

83
architectural features

Architectural features are generally found in older homes and add interest to a room, though such features can also be added to homes of a later date providing it is done with care and with an eye to the proportions of the room. When it comes to decorating, your choice of colour can further enhance these features.

For example, columns or pilasters were often employed to exaggerate the height of a room or were sometimes placed on either side of a tall window or French doors to frame a view. You can make a feature of such columns by painting them in a contrasting colour to the walls, and maybe adding a touch of gilt embellishment. Alternatively, you could paint them to look like marble, which was often how they were treated in the eighteenth and nineteenth centuries.

Lintels and pediments made of wood or stone were sometimes used to frame doors and windows or grace the top of an archway. They can be simple, thick bands or ornately carved, like the classical broken pediment. If these features are in stone it is usually best to leave them in their natural but cleaned state. If they are of wood, they may be painted or left unpainted.

A sweeping staircase, whether traditional or modern, is a magnificent feature in its own right. A modern one might be made of wood, stone, glass, metal, concrete or a combination of materials. Each of these materials will impart its own intrinsic colour and will not need any further enhancement.

A traditional staircase can be made even more dramatic if its treads are carpeted with a runner in a rich colour to contrast with the treads and the wall; for example, if the walls are in a patterned, predominantly green wallpaper, use a rich burgundy red carpet with brass stair rods over a dark, mahogany-stained wooden floor and stairs.

top tip

Architectural features are usually old and may have suffered from years of over-painting, which will dull or conceal the definition of the pattern or form, or they may have suffered from the combined effects of neglect and central heating. Investigation, maintenance and restoration should be a priority before any additional colour or finishes are applied.

84

woodwork

As with architectural features (see 83) you should establish whether your colour scheme is best enhanced by natural, unpainted woodwork or by having the woodwork painted. A paint finish will provide some protection against wear and tear, but natural wood can be treated and sealed with matt or gloss varnish to protect the surface.

If you opt for painted woodwork, you don't necessarily have to use the same colour everywhere. Doors and shutters with panels, for instance, could have their panels or the beadwork picked out in a colour that complements or contrasts with the room scheme, rather than matches the rest of the woodwork. You could select the colour from a fabric or pattern used in the room.

five ways to decorate woodwork

1 • Use white. This is the classic choice, and will contrast with any colour or pattern of wall, except, of course, a white one. The 'frame' provided by a white-painted skirting acts as a dividing line between the floor and wall and has the effect of seeming to reduce wall height. If you want a more subtle effect, you could opt for off-white.

2 • Use the wall colour, which has the effect of making the wall seem larger.

3 • Use a contrasting colour. By using a paint in a shade lighter or darker than the wall you can lessen the impact of any woodwork but still acknowledge its presence. Black is an especially dramatic choice, particularly against walls in a strong colour such as red or yellow.

4 • Stay natural. You can strip the woodwork back to its original state and protect it with a clear varnish or wax finish. Varnish is more resilient but wax or oil will soak into the wood, giving a pleasant, matt appearance.

5 • Use faux effects for plain or featureless woodwork, particularly pine, which is usually pale and less knotted or featured than other woods. You could use graining to imitate the grain of a more expensive wood, or you could marble it to make it look like any one of the many beautifully coloured marbles.

part three

keeping it fresh

94 dyeing fabrics

There comes a time when a fabric can start to look jaded. Depending on the fabric type, it can be revitalised by dyeing. Even carpets can be spruced up with a careful application of a cold-water dye.

• Coffee and tea can be used to give an aged or antique tint to white or off-white natural textiles such as cotton or linen. The colour result will be deeper and stronger the longer you leave the fabric submerged.

• To achieve an ombré or gradual shading effect, dye the whole piece first for a few moments, then gradually lift the fabric from the dye so that the next section is submerged for longer and so becomes darker. Repeat the process so that the last section of material will have been in the dye the longest and is a deep rich tone whereas the first section is a pale pastel shade.

• Tie-dye patterns can be achieved by tying sections of cloth very tightly with cotton string. Dip the tied cloth into the dyestuff and leave it until it is well soaked. Rinse and dry the cloth, then cut off the cotton ties. The areas that were tied up so that they were not exposed to the dye will retain their original colour. The cloth can be re-tied and dyed again to create areas of yet another colour.

freshen up a wall with colour

95

Just as fabrics can become tired-looking, so walls can get scuffed and worn, or you may simply be bored with their colour. Rather than repaint a whole wall, you could use a toning or contrasting colour to add some pattern or a motif on top of the existing wall colour.

three fresh ideas

1 • A horizontal band of contrasting colour above the skirting and at the top of the wall will create a frame for the wall as well as introducing another colour.
2 • Paint vertical stripes over the existing base colour or, for a more daring scheme, try polka dots, using either a stencil or a saucer or dish as a template.
3 • Sponge or rag-roll a fresh new colour on top. Try a deeper shade of the existing colour for a subtle but rejuvenating effect, for example terracotta over an apricot base or pastel green over white.

alcoves etc.

If you have a feature such as an alcove or recess, painting or papering it in a different colour will instantly revitalise the look of the room. If you use a colour that contrasts with the walls, such as cadmium red with white walls, or pale grey with yellow walls, the feature will become the room's fresh new focus.

96

add a colour, change your mood

If you want a change of mood, but not a complete colour makeover, all you have to do is add another colour to your existing palette, perhaps in the shape of a set of new accessories such as a throw, some new curtains and a rug, new loose covers or cushions, or some bedlinen or towels for kitchen or bathroom. The results can be dramatic and for relatively little cost.

from lively to sombre

A lively palette of fresh green, beige and sunflower yellow can be made more sombre and earthy with the addition of a tan colour and some woody browns. The original lively palette has earthy connotations; its colours could have been selected from any of a number of flower blossoms, so the browns you add, which share the yellow base of both the fresh green and the sunflower yellow are a fitting accompaniment.

pastels get some zip

A pastel palette of white, pale rose and dove grey will be given some zip if you add a touch of black. This combination of colours is reminiscent of the grand settings and costumes of Cecil Beaton's designs for the film 'My Fair Lady'. The colours work very well in a mixture of plains and stripes.

tone down the fire

Fiery, fluo-bright pink and green can be toned down by adding matt black or large areas of matt white. The matt finish will help the dampening effect of the black or white and in some cases a combination of both, say a black floor with white walls, will create a background that mutes and distances the vivid colours.

wistful gets edgy

Wistful sage and beige become more edgy with orange. Sage green is a blue-green which is opposite orange on the colour wheel (see 1). Sage green and orange also share a base colour of yellow.

97 change the floor, change the colour

If you have an existing hard floor you can change its appearance by adding a colourful rug or mat, for example a dark wood or grey stone floor can be 'lifted' when a large, central area is covered with a red-dyed coir mat or a thick-pile, colourfully patterned Chinese carpet.

If you have a bland wall-to-wall carpet, this can also be partially concealed by overlaying it with a mat. In this case a thin cotton dhurrie or kelim will be more appropriate than a thick carpet-style rug. If the carpet itself has seen better days, lift it up and throw it away, then sand and varnish your floor to give your room a whole new look.

move the furniture 98

By moving the furniture around and re-arranging it into different groups or pairings you can change the appearance and colour emphasis of a room. For example, if you have two armchairs upholstered in red placed in front of a window where they can be seen when you walk into the room, their lively, bright colour will be a bold, eye-catching introduction to the space. But move them to an alcove or to somewhere where they aren't seen as soon as you enter the room, and replace them with a two-seater sofa of similar dimensions to the two chairs. Then upholster the sofa in a muted mustard colour and add a couple of aubergine-coloured suede cushions, and the room will suddenly look far more relaxed and easy-going.

A rug or floor covering can have a similar effect. If you have taupe-coloured walls, pale wood floors and a buff-coloured, sandstone fire surround, then a russet red mat in front of the hearth will draw the eye to the fireplace and its surround. But if you move the mat and place it in front of a desk or under a coffee table, the fireplace will become less of a feature and the eye-catching colour of the mat will draw the attention to the desk or coffee table instead.

99 cleaning hard surfaces

Keeping surfaces clean is essential to ensuring that their colours stay looking fresh and bright.

wooden floors

Wooden floors will eventually lose their gloss with constant wear, but this can be revived by polishing. Depending on the existing surface treatment, you may need to strip or remove the wax or oil before applying a new coat. A fresh application of wax may have to be left for a while to soak into the surface of the wood, before buffing and shining.

lino and synthetic floors

Linoleum and other synthetic floors are usually adequately cleaned with a wet floor mop and proprietary cleaner, but for certain top-of-the-range synthetic floors, a liquid seal may be necessary to give a high-gloss, durable finish.

laminates

These are best maintained with a wipe of a soapy sponge or cloth. Dry with a cloth or kitchen towel.

steel

This may be durable but it should be treated with care; wire wool and abrasive cleaners will scratch the surface and make it appear cloudy. If you use a smooth cream cleaner, buff up the surface afterwards with baby oil; this will give a shiny lustre without leaving residue.

wooden furniture

The sheen of a well-polished piece of wood adds richness to its colour, but wood requires regular attention, especially in homes with central heating, which can dry it out. For everyday care, all you need is a good regular bi-annual or annual waxing, depending on the amount of use the furniture gets. And, if there are upholstered panels or seats, you should occasionally tap or beat these to remove dust and any crumbs.

stone

Most stone, such as polished marble and granite, will revive with gentle washing with soap and water and buffing with a soft cloth or chamois, but if the stone has an oil or wax surface finish, you should follow the maintenance advice given by the supplier or fitter.

glass

Whether clear, opaque or coloured, glass can be cleaned with a tablespoon of vinegar diluted in water and applied with a clean, lint-free cloth. Some people use the old-fashioned method of a roll of damp newspaper to clean larger surface areas of glass and there are also many sprays and aerosol products, specially formulated for glass cleaning, on the market. Coloured glass especially, looks more vivid, intense and brilliant when it is clean.

paintwork

For standard gloss, eggshell, matt and vinyl finishes, a damp cloth with a small amount of cream cleaner is usually all that is required to remove marks and brighten up the colour, but chalky and limewash finishes should not be brought into contact with water. The best way to revive these finishes is to repaint them.

100 cleaning soft surfaces

The cleaning of soft surfaces shouldn't present any problems if you match the surface to the treatment and cleaning product.

carpets

Fitted carpets benefit from thorough, regular vacuum cleaning. They should also be shampooed from time to time. Specialist commercial shampoo products and machines, often available for hire through dry cleaners, DIY stores and hire shops, produce a light foam. This cleans the surface of the carpet without drenching the backing. The foam may either be removed while it is still damp using the cleaning machine or, in some cases, the foam dries to a powder which can easily be removed by using a conventional vacuum cleaner.

natural floor coverings

Natural floor coverings don't respond well to water so should not be washed. Instead clean them thoroughly with a vacuum cleaner. If the floor covering has a prominent weave, you will need to adjust the suction of the vacuum accordingly. Use a nozzle fitting rather than running a heavy upright over the surface as this may flatten the weave.

rugs and mats

Rugs may be taken outside and thoroughly beaten which will remove loose fibres and ingrained dust, but for a more thorough clean they should be taken to a good dry cleaner. If the rug or mat is cotton, check on the label and see if it can be machine- or hand-washed.

leather

Leather can become dry and dull so needs to be 'fed' regularly with a specialist oil or wax to keep its gloss and suppleness. Leather and suede both benefit from a gentle brushing with a soft bristle brush to remove surface grime.

curtains and upholstery

Always determine whether a fabric is washable by reading the instructions on the label or on the selvage. If you are in doubt, consult a specialist cleaner. If all else fails, try a small test patch, on a hem or inner seam, to see if water or detergent has any adverse effect.

101

wash the windows – let the light in

index

acknowledgements

All photography by Ray Main/ Mainstream except those by Darren Chung/Mainstream (pages 14, 17, 32, 53, 68 & 114).

Design by: 7 Architect Glyn Emrys; 19 Designer Ozwald Boatang; 22 Design by Filer & Cox; D'Squared design; 25 Architect Peter Wadley; 26 Designer Matt Livesy

Hammond; 28 Pearl Lowe; 30 Design Karen Howes; 31 Designer www.shaunclarkeson.com; 32 Architecture & Design Association; 38 Inside Design Company; 47 Designer Joseph; 49 Designer Fleur Rossdale; Architect Gregory Phillips; 52 Architect Gregory Phillips; 60 designer Ben De Lisi; 61

Guinivere; 67 Architect Simon Conder; 69 Designer Drew Plunkett; Designer Peter Wadley; 72 Designer Alidad; 75 Designer David Tansley; 76 Eltham Place; 77 Designer Peter Kent/Architect Wells Cote; 78 Peter Wadley Architects; 78–9 Flying Duck Enterprises; 86 Barratta Design; 87 Designer Matt

Livesy Hammond; 92 Designer Claire Nash; 95 The Inside Design Studios; 98 kbjarchitectects.co.uk; 99 Peter Wadley Architects; 102 Babylon Design; 103 Architect Zeynep Fadillioglu; 104 20th Century Design; 106 Arch Nico Rensch; 107 Mark Smith Creative; 112 Hemmingway Designs.